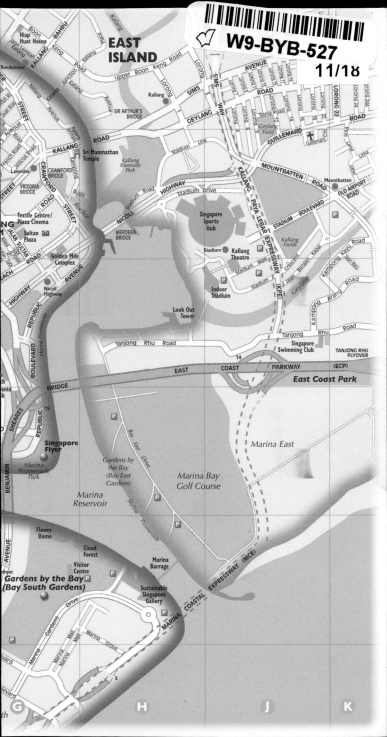

Fodor's
25 Best

SINGAPORE

How to Use This Book

KEY TO SYMBOLS

✚ Map reference to the accompanying fold-out map

✉ Address

☎ Telephone number

🕐 Opening/closing times

🍴 Restaurant or café

🚉 Nearest rail station

Ⓜ Nearest MRT station

🚌 Nearest bus route

🛳 Nearest riverboat or ferry stop

♿ Facilities for visitors with disabilities

❓ Other practical information

▷ Further information

ℹ Tourist information

✋ Admission charges: Expensive (over S$30), Moderate (S$11–S$30), and Inexpensive (S$10 or less)

This guide is divided into four sections

● Essential Singapore: An introduction to the city and tips on making the most of your stay.
● Singapore by Area: We've broken the city into four areas, and recommended the best sights, shops, entertainment venues, nightlife and restaurants in each one. Suggested walks help you to explore on foot.
● Where to Stay: The best hotels, whether you're looking for luxury, budget or something in between.
● Need to Know: The info you need to make your trip run smoothly, including getting about by public transportation, weather tips, emergency phone numbers and useful websites.

Navigation In the Singapore by Area chapter, we've given each area its own tint, which is also used on the locator maps throughout the book and the map on the inside front cover.

Maps The fold-out map with this book is a comprehensive street plan of central Singapore. The grid on this map is the same as the grid on The City area locator map and has upper-case grid references. Sights and listings within the East Island and West Island areas have lower-case grid references.

Contents

Introducing Singapore

The tiny island nation of Singapore is a dramatic fusion of the Victorian age and the 21st century. From its sweeping skyscrapers and pretty colonial architecture to world-class dining for every budget, the Lion City is guaranteed to impress.

Tree-lined avenues, landscaped urban areas, small parks and lush roadside tropical greenery are common features of this attractive, tidy city. Building on an illustrious trading history, Singapore is the world's busiest shipping port, and rivaled only by Tokyo as Asia's premier financial hub. Despite the island's impressive development, seen in the cityscape of tower blocks, freeways and glitzy malls, Singapore retains a fairly laid-back feel and pockets of the old world remain in superbly restored (or occasionally rebuilt) areas.

The diversity of race—Chinese, Malay, Indians, plus workers from other parts of Asia and the West—and the myriad religions, festivals and cultural practices is where Singapore sets itself apart. Ancient imported traditions remain important but a strong Singaporean identity has been forged in the country's rapid development, and relations between the races are better than in many other cosmopolitan cities.

Lying just over 60 miles (100km) north of the equator, the island has a tropical climate and high year-round humidity that saps the energy of most locals and visitors alike, particularly in the afternoon. Fortunately most public facilities are frigidly air-conditioned.

From the colorful temples of Chinatown and bustling markets of Little India, to the shisha cafés of Kampong Glam and shopping frenzy of Orchard Road, every Singapore neighborhood has its own distinct character and charm. So board a bus, hop on the MRT, or wander the sidewalks on foot to explore the many delights of this vibrant island republic.

FACTS AND FIGURES

● Population in 1819: 1,000; population in 2017: 5.6 million
● Religions: Buddhist 34%; Muslim 14%; Taoist 11%; Catholic 7%; Hindu 5%; other/none 29%
● Ethnic Groups: Chinese 74%; Malay 13%; Indian 9%; other 4%
● Official languages: English, Malay, Mandarin Chinese, Tamil

SINGLISH

You're bound to hear Singlish, the local colloquial English, spoken by many Singaporeans. It's a blend of English and Hokkien (the local Chinese language), Malay and Tamil. You'll know someone is using it if they frequently use the word *lah* to show emphasis. Other common Singlish words and phrases include: *fli-end* (friend), *tok kong* (very good) and *lerf* (love).

A FINE CITY

You may have heard that Singapore is a fine city (you can even buy the T-shirt). The government's perfectly reasonable campaign to keep the city clean, and its citizens socially responsible, includes imposing fines of up to S$1,000 for such acts as littering, jaywalking or even failure to flush a public toilet.

SURROUNDING ISLANDS

While Singapore's best-known island is the recreational Sentosa (▷ 64–65), once a British fort, the country is surrounded by more than 50 small islands. They're mostly occupied by the military, oil refineries or nature reserves, but St. John's Island (▷ 98) is a picnic destination, and Kusu Island (▷ 100) has a turtle sanctuary.

A Short Stay in Singapore

DAY 1

Morning Have an early breakfast and head for the **Singapore Botanic Gardens** (▷ 66–67), the world's only tropical garden to earn UNESCO World Heritage Site recognition. Only a few minutes' bus ride from Orchard Road, this expansive green space is best explored in the morning. Watch out for monitor lizards!

Mid-morning Take a bus or taxi back into the city for a stroll along **Orchard Road** (▷ 38–39). It's less crowded before noon, and you can always come back later to do a little more than window-shopping.

Lunch Make your way to **Chinatown** (▷ 27) for an authentic Singaporean-style lunch among locals at a hawker center (open-air food court). **Chinatown Complex Food Centre** (▷ 28) is one of the best.

Afternoon Wander Chinatown's atmospheric backstreets, where you'll find all sorts of local boutiques and food shops. Be sure to visit the **Chinatown Heritage Centre** (▷ 27) and the impressive **Buddha Tooth Relic Temple** (▷ 26).

Mid-afternoon Hop in a taxi to beat the afternoon heat inside the **Asian Civilisations Museum** (▷ 24–25), which features a vast collection of artwork, housed in a beautifully restored colonial-period building.

Dinner Cross Cavenagh Bridge and enjoy a riverside meal at one of the lively bars and restaurants along Boat Quay.

Evening Head back across the Singapore River to **Merlion Park** on Marina Bay (▷ 35), the sparkling heart of the city. The views of the futuristic Marina Bay Sands hotel, spiked Esplanade Theatres, and lotus-shaped ArtScience Museum at night are spectacular.

DAY 2

Morning Start the day like a local with a strong coffee and *kaya* (coconut jam) toast at one of the many *kopitiams* (coffee shops) likely to be near your hotel. Afterwards take a walk through historic **Raffles Hotel** (▷ 40); from there it's a short walk to **National Gallery Singapore** (▷ 36), home to the world's largest collection of modern Southeast Asian art.

Mid-morning Head to frenetic **Little India** (▷ 33), where you can spend hours exploring the winding lanes and alleyways lined with pastel-colored shophouses and teeming with interesting sights.

Lunch Refuel with a delicious North or South Indian lunch at whichever of the many restaurants in Little India strike your fancy. Why not try **Komala Vilas** (▷ 53) or **The Banana Leaf Apolo** (▷ 52).

Afternoon Make a beeline for **Gardens by the Bay** (▷ 30–31), with the oft-photographed Supertree Grove, Flower Dome and Cloud Forest.

Mid-afternoon Catch the MRT from Bayfront to **Clarke Quay** (▷ 29). Explore the shops around Clarke Quay and perhaps take a boat ride on the Singapore River.

Dinner Clarke Quay may be a little touristy, but its bars and restaurants are still packed nightly, and it's a fun place to settle in for a while. There are any number of restaurants from which to choose, but go to **Motorino** (▷ 29) for New York-style pizza or **Violet Oon Satay Bar & Grill** (▷ 54) for upscale Peranakan.

Evening End the evening with some locally brewed craft beers at **Brewerkz** (▷ 50), just across the river. It's Singapore's oldest brewpub and still one of the best.

Top 25

► ► ►

Asian Civilisations Museum ▷ 24–25 Asian history and culture meet in this stunning building.

Buddha Tooth Relic Temple and Museum ▷ 26 The city's most important Buddhist site.

Chinatown ▷ 27 Enjoy gorgeous shophouses, buzzing restaurants and sprawling markets.

Singapore Zoo and River Safari ▷ 70–71 Award-winning zoo and river-themed safari park.

Singapore Nature Reserves ▷ 68–69 Escape the city to tropical open spaces.

Singapore Flyer ▷ 42 There are spectacular views across Singapore from the world's tallest observation wheel.

Singapore Botanic Gardens ▷ 66–67 Superbly landscaped gardens full of tropical plants.

Singapore Art Museum ▷ 41 Local and Asian art is beautifully displayed at this state-of-the-art gallery.

Sentosa ▷ 64–65 An island playground reached via a fabulous cable-car ride.

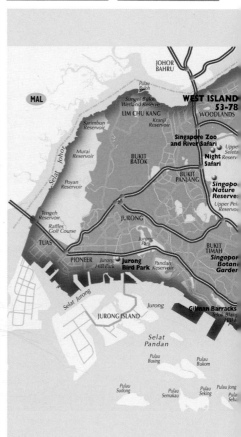

Raffles Hotel ▷ 40 Experience colonial-era style at its grandest in this historic luxury hotel.

Pulau Ubin ▷ 96–97 Get away from it all at this sleepy offshore island enclave.

Orchard Road ▷ 38–39 Eat and shop to your heart's content at the city's glitzy megamalls.

These pages are a quick guide to the Top 25, which are described in more detail later. Here they are listed alphabetically, and the tinted background shows which area they are in.

Chinatown Complex Food Centre ▷ 28
Eat your way through this labyrinthine food court.

Clarke Quay ▷ 29
Wine, dine and dance at one of the most popular nightlife destinations.

East Coast Park ▷ 84–85
Running and biking trails, beachside seafood shacks and ample picnic areas.

Gardens by the Bay ▷ 30–31 The Supertrees and Cloud Forest are the stars at this futuristic park.

Gillman Barracks ▷ 58–59 Singapore's cutting-edge art galleries at restored colonial barracks.

Jurong Bird Park ▷ 60–61 Marvel at the more than 5,000 birds from around the world.

Kampong Glam ▷ 32
Go shopping in this handsome historic district.

Little India ▷ 33 The sights, sounds and smells of India come to life on these lively city streets.

Marina Bay Sands ▷ 34
An iconic part of the cityscape, this integrated resort is dedicated to leisure.

Merlion Park ▷ 35 The iconic fish-tailed lion overlooks Marina Bay.

Night Safari ▷ 62–63
Hop on a tram for an evening ride through this park to see myriad exotic animals.

National Museum of Singapore ▷ 37
Singapore's history comes to life here.

National Gallery Singapore ▷ 36 Superb collection of modern Southeast Asian art.

THE CITY
1 Singapore Art Museum
2 National Museum of Singapore
3 Chinatown Complex Food Centre
4 Buddha Tooth Relic Temple and Museum
5 Asian Civilisations Museum
6 Merlion Park

MAL

EMBAWANG
Pulau Seletar
Selat
Johor
Pulau Punggol Barat
Pulau Punggol Timor

SHUN
Yishun Park
Orchid Country Club
Lower Seletar Reservoir

EAST ISLAND 79–92 PUNGGOL
Pulau Serangoon
Pulau Ubin
Pulau Ketam
Pulau Ubin Park
Serangoon Harbour

ANG MO KIO
SENGKANG
HOUGANG
PASIR RIS
Pasir Ris Park
CHANGI

MacRitchie Reservoir
BISHAN
SERANGOON
Bedok Reservoir
SIMEI

TOA PAYOH
CHANGI EAST

THE CITY 21–52
Orchard Road
LITTLE KAMPONG
INDIA GLAM
BEDOK

Clarke Quay
HINATOWN
Raffles Hotel
National Gallery Singapore
Singapore Flyer
Gardens by the Bay
Marina Bay Sands
East Coast Park

Pulau Brani
Sentosa
Pulau Tekukor
Pulau Seringat
Pulau Tembakul (Kusu Island)
Pulau Darat
Pulau Lazarus (Sakijang Pelepah)
Pulau Sakijang Bendera (St John's Island)
Pulau Subar Laut (Sisters' Islands)

◄ ◄ ◄

Shopping

Shopping is serious business in Singapore, arguably Southeast Asia's retail capital. Indeed, the endless shops may seem to outnumber residents.

What to Look For

Orchard Road (▷ 38–39) provides a comprehensive shopping experience on a par with world capitals, and is particularly recommended for brand-name fashion, electronics and home decor. A particular pleasure in Singapore is visiting the many specialist shops, especially those located in Chinatown, Little India, and other ethnic areas. Chinese goods, for instance, include ornately decorated porcelain, masks, silk and traditional paintings, while baskets, ikat cloth, batiks, puppets, sarongs and leatherware are among the Malay goods. Jewelry, sculptures and pottery abound in Little India.

Shopping Areas

Not surprisingly, given Singapore's hot and humid weather, all large buildings are very well air-conditioned. Major Orchard Road department stores include Tangs, Robinsons and Takashimaya. Be sure to check out Far East Plaza in Scotts Road for on-trend fashions. For small, inexpensive souvenirs, take the MRT to Bugis. For cameras and electronic equipment, try Lucky Plaza or Sim Lim Square, armed with your STB good retailers guide (▷ 11). The huge Marina Square Mall, which includes Millenia Walk and is five minutes' walk from Raffles City MRT station, has lots of homeware shops. Chinatown has a mix of souvenir and antiques shops, including the rough-and-tumble

DUTY-FREE LAWS

Singapore's Tourist Refund Scheme means you can claim back 7 percent Goods and Services Tax on large purchases when you depart from Changi Airport. Whenever you spend more than S$100 with a single retailer in a single day, ask for a copy of the GST tax refund form and present it to airport customs officials to claim your refund.

Clockwise from top: Marina Bay Sands; lanterns for sale for Mid-Autumn Festival;

People's Park Complex, which is a local favorite and throwback to Singapore retailing circa the 1960s. In the colonial district try the lovely CHIJMES mall and nearby Raffles City for fashion and food. Antiques lovers should check out Tanglin Mall, while the Paragon Shopping Centre and ION Orchard are two of Singapore's most high-end shopping malls. In Little India, the gargantuan Mustafa Centre is open 24 hours a day, seven days a week, and would take days to fully explore. As you would expect, Singapore's retail blitz continues to evolve in exciting ways—though in some cases, the old suffers at the expense of the new. Shopping has become such a lifestyle activity that destinations such as VivoCity and Marina Bay Sands meld entertainment with shopping in architecturally stimulating surroundings, with their lush parks, promenades and children's play areas.

Markets
Following the closure of the long-running outdoor Thieves Market, the weekly flea market at China Square Central Mall on Sundays is one of the last bric-a-brac markets of its kind left.

Haggling
While bargaining in the markets and suburban shops is considered part of the Singapore experience, and most electronic stores and jewelers expect it, brand-name boutiques and department stores have fixed, clearly marked prices.

CONSUMER PROTECTION

The Singapore government is very keen to promote hassle-free, safe shopping for consumers. To aid and protect shoppers, the STB (Singapore Tourism Board) publishes a shopping guide (available at tourism offices) which lists good retailers—those preferred retailers chosen for their service and reliability—and a list of retailers to avoid. A special hotline number, 1800 736 2000, has been set up to assist tourists who have had bad retail experiences during their stay in Singapore. You can also email your comments to feedback@stb.com.sg.

shopping in Chinatown; the famous Orchard Road; elephant ornaments in Little India

Shopping by Theme

Whether you're looking for a department store, a quirky boutique or something in between, you'll find it all in Singapore. On this page shops are listed by theme. For a more detailed write-up, see the individual listings in Singapore by Area.

Antiques and Handicrafts
Antiques of the Orient (▷ 79)
Mata Hari Antiques (▷ 48)
Rumah Bebe (▷ 90)

Books
BooksActually (▷ 79)
Books Kinokuniya, in Ngee Ann (▷ 49)

Department Stores
Tangs (▷ 50)
Yue Hwa Chinese Products Emporium (▷ 50)

Design and Gifts
Strangelets (▷ 79)

Shopping Malls and Streets
112 Katong (▷ 90)
313@Somerset (▷ 48)
Arab Street (▷ 43)

Bugis Junction (▷ 43)
Bugis Street (▷ 43)
Centrepoint (▷ 48)
Century Square and Tampines Mall (▷ 90)
Changi City Point (▷ 90)
Chinatown Point (▷ 48)
City Plaza (▷ 90)
Clarke Quay (▷ 29)
Geylang Serai (▷ 90)
ION Orchard (▷ 48)
Johor Bahru Duty Free Complex (ZON) (▷ 106)
Lucky Plaza (▷ 48)
Mandarin Gallery (▷ 48)
Millenia Walk (▷ 48)
Mustafa Centre (▷ 49)
Ngee Ann City (▷ 49)
Orchard Central (▷ 49)
Orchard Road (▷ 38–39)
Paragon (▷ 49)
Parkway Parade (▷ 90)
People's Park Complex (▷ 49)
Plaza Pelangi (▷ 106)

Raffles City (▷ 49)
Resorts World Sentosa Luxury Fashion Galleria (▷ 79)
Suntec City Mall (▷ 49)
Tanglin Mall (▷ 79)
Tanglin Shopping Centre (▷ 79)
Tanjungpinang City Center (▷ 106)
Temple/Pagoda/ Trengganu Streets (▷ 50)
VivoCity (▷ 79)

Singapore by Night

There's no shortage of things to do in Singapore after the sun goes down, from night safaris to heaving after-hours clubs.

Stepping Out

Singapore is certainly a late-night destination. Many retail stores stay open until 9 or 10pm, some hawker centers never close and many bars and clubs stay packed into the wee morning hours. Reliably active after-hours locations include Orchard Road (particularly around Emerald Hill); Boat, Robertson and Clarke quays; Chinatown (Ann Siang Hill and Keong Saik); and the Civic District. There's always some action in Little India and around Bugis Street as well, and many Western expats frequent Holland Village.

Riverside Action

A reliable choice for those new to town is to head for the Boat Quay or Clarke Quay (▷ 29) districts. Both areas have ample bars, clubs and restaurants to choose from, and a laid-back, fun-loving riverside ambience. Alternatively, take an evening cruise down the Singapore River to get a different perspective of the city and its fascinating architecture, or party with locals at one of the many late-night cocktail bars, craft beer taprooms or nightclubs.

Open All Hours

There is a glut of after-dark attractions in the city. You can go on safari, go for a bike ride, play golf or make a bungee jump long after dusk. Gardens by the Bay (▷ 30–31) puts on a spectacular light show every evening. The Southern Ridges walkway (▷ 75–76) is also brilliantly lit for a late-night stroll.

DRINKING OUT

To get the night off to a good start, and to help compensate for Singapore's noticeably high drink prices, take advantage of the happy hours that are typically available at most bars from around 5pm until 8pm.

From top: downtown; dance floor at 1-Altitude; live music; outdoor dining; Boat Quay

Where to Eat

Nothing reflects Singapore's vibrant society
and diverse ethnicities more than its incredible range of cuisine.

Hawker Centers
Hawker centers offer the quintessential
Singaporean food experience and should top all
travelers' to-do lists. Hawker centers are like
open-air food courts (though some of them are
actually indoors), where talented, tireless cooks
serve their unique specialties hot, fresh and
cheap. The centers vary in size, but often house
upward of 50 vendors.

Regional Cuisine
Dishes from Malaysia, India, Thailand, China
and Indonesia are most prevalent, though don't
be surprised to see some hawker stalls serving
Singaporean-style Western food, too. Tiny restaurants tucked away on side streets in places
like Chinatown and Little India are also great
places to get tasty, affordable and authentic
foods. You can try Malay Muslim or Indian
Muslim fare. Known as "Mamak" food, you
will know where to go to get this by looking
for the restaurant signs written in Arabic.

Fine Dining
At the other end of the food spectrum,
Singapore's fine-dining scene is one of Asia's
best. Dempsey Hill, Marina Bay Sands and
Keong Saik Road are all home to numerous
high-end restaurants well worth the splurge.

HAND OR CUTLERY?

Many Hindus and Muslims eat their food with the right
hand only; it is considered unclean to eat with the left
hand, although it's okay to use utensils—usually a fork
and spoon. Eating with your hand, you tear pieces of
chapati (using only one hand) and then soak or scoop up
elements of the meal. For rice there's another technique:
you add the curries and work up the mixture into balls,
which you then pick up and pop—almost flick—into
your mouth.

From top: classic chicken
and rice; Robertson
Quay; Dempsey Hill;
chef at work

Where to Eat by Cuisine

There are plenty of places to eat to suit all tastes and budgets in Singapore. On this page they are listed by cuisine. For a more detailed description of each venue, see Singapore by Area.

Asian
Banyan Tree Bintan (▷ 106)
Indochine (▷ 53)

BBQ
Burnt Ends (▷ 52)
Smokey's BBQ (▷ 92)

Brewpubs
Brewerkz (▷ 50)
LeVel 33 (▷ 51)
RedDot BrewHouse (▷ 80)

British
Bread Street Kitchen (▷ 52)
Rabbit Carrot Gun (▷ 92)

Chinese
Beng Thin Hoon Kee (▷ 52)
Crystal Jade (▷ 53)
New Hong Kong Restaurant (▷ 106)
Yum Cha (▷ 54)

Coffee and Dessert
2am:dessertbar (▷ 80)
FATCAT Ice Cream Bar (▷ 92)
O'Coffee Club (▷ 80)
Raffles Hotel (▷ 40)

European Fusion
The Coastal Settlement (▷ 92)
Cure (▷ 53)
Kilo (▷ 53)
Restaurant André (▷ 54)

Hawker Centers
Chinatown Complex Food Centre (▷ 28)
Chinatown Food Street (▷ 52)
East Coast Lagoon Food Centre (▷ 92)
Lau Pa Sat (▷ 53)
Taman Sri Tebrau Hawker Centre (▷ 106)

Indian
The Banana Leaf Apolo (▷ 52)
Komala Vilas (▷ 53)
Rang Mahal (▷ 54)
Samy's Curry (▷ 80)

Italian
Pasta Brava (▷ 54)
Prego (▷ 54)

Peranakan
Blue Ginger (▷ 52)
Candlenut (▷ 80)
National Kitchen by Violet Oon (▷ 54)

Seafood
Jumbo Seafood (▷ 92)
Long Beach (▷ 80)
The Naked Finn (▷ 80)
No Signboard Seafood (▷ 92)
Season Live Seafood (▷ 106)

Spanish
Blu Kouzina (▷ 80)
Dempsey Cookhouse and Bar (▷ 80)
Esquina (▷ 53)
Lolla (▷ 53)

Vegetarian
Supernature (▷ 54)

Top Tips For…

These great suggestions will help you tailor your ideal visit to Singapore, no matter how you choose to spend your time. Each sight or listing has a fuller write-up elsewhere.

LEARNING ABOUT LOCAL CULTURE

Start at the National Museum of Singapore (▷ 37) then visit the nearby Asian Civilisations Museum (▷ 24–25) and the comprehensive Singapore Art Museum (▷ 41).

Don't miss the National Gallery Singapore (▷ 36), which houses the world's largest collection of modern Southeast Asian and Singaporean art.

Head to Little India (▷ 33) or Chinatown (▷ 27) for a lively slice of everyday life in Singapore; both are busy day and night and great places to shop, snack and sightsee.

RETAIL PURSUITS

Start on Orchard Road (▷ 38–39), where ION Orchard and high-end Paragon Shopping Centre are just two of the labyrinthine megamalls and department stores worth exploring.

In Tiong Bahru, BooksActually (▷ 79) is an indie-minded bookshop offering works by local and international authors, as well as a vintage bric-a-brac section in the back that's fun to pick through.

The behemoth Mustafa Centre, a 24-hour shopping center in Little India (▷ 49), stocks just about anything you can possibly imagine.

FINE DINING

At The Shoppes at Marina Bay Sands, take your pick of celebrity chef-owned restaurants that include Gordon Ramsey's Bread Street Kitchen (▷ 52), a modern British gastropub with views of the bay.

Restaurant André (▷ 54) in Chinatown offers some of the most sought-after tables in Singapore. It's pricey, but this singular dining experience is worth the splurge.

Head to National Kitchen by Violet Oon (▷ 54) at the National Gallery for exceptional Peranakan cuisine served in one of Singapore's classiest dining rooms.

Clockwise from top left: hawker center dining; Marina Bay Sands; Clarke Quay; Resorts

HITTING THE HAWKER CENTERS

Chinatown Complex Food Centre (▷ 28) is home to Hong Kong Soya Sauce Chicken Rice and Noodle, the world's most affordable Michelin-starred restaurant.

Lau Pa Sat (▷ 53), the venerable *grande dame* of Singapore's hawker centers, is one of the prettiest as well as busiest in the city.

SIPPING CRAFT BEERS

Located in a gorgeous Chinese shophouse in up-and-coming Jalan Besar, Druggists (▷ 51) is a friendly spot serving 23 taps of rare craft beers from around the world.

Good Luck Beerhouse (▷ 51), on Haji Lane in Kampong Glam, is a great place to try locally brewed craft beers on draft.

Pair your hawker food feast with craft beers at Smith Street Taps (▷ 51), on the second floor of the Chinatown Complex.

Brewerkz (▷ 50), directly opposite Clarke Quay, is Singapore's oldest brewpub.

DINNER AND DRINKS

Clarke Quay (▷ 29) offers a wide range of bars, restaurants and nightclubs, and the riverside setting is particularly lovely after sunset.

On and around Keong Saik Road in Chinatown, the bars and restaurants have forged one of Singapore's hottest nightlife scenes. Cure (▷ 53) and Esquina (▷ 53) are area highlights.

SKY-HIGH CITY VIEWS

At Marina Bay Sands, CÉ LA VIE (▷ 51) offers a stylish setting for views from the hotel's 57th-floor rooftop deck.

The Singapore Flyer (▷ 42) is one of the world's tallest Ferris wheels and offers the views that come with such a distinction.

Get one of the best bird's-eye views of Singapore's glittering downtown area at LeVeL33 (▷ 51), which bills itself as the "world's highest urban craft brewery."

The OCBC Skyway (▷ 30) offers great views over the Supertree Grove in Gardens by the Bay.

World, Sentosa; colorful shutters, Little India; Bugis Junction; Chinese New Year feast

ENTERTAINING THE KIDS

Take them to Sentosa (▷ 64–65): with a water park, cable-car ride to/from Mount Faber, beaches and Universal Studios, there's plenty to do.

The Singapore Science Centre (▷ 75) has a number of fun interactive exhibits.

At Gardens by the Bay (▷ 30–31), kids will love running wild at the Children's Garden and exploring the Supertree Grove on an aerial walkway.

A POSH NIGHT OUT

Stylish Post Bar at the Fullerton Hotel (▷ 112) serves classic cocktails in elegant surroundings.

Award-winning Manhattan (▷ 51), located at Regent Singapore, is one of the most highly rated bars in all of Asia.

For cocktails under the stars, head to 1-Altitude (▷ 50), the highest rooftop bar in the Lion City.

CONNECT WITH NATURE

Start early or late to avoid the midday heat for a walk along the trails of Bukit Timah (▷ 68), a surviving patch of primary tropical rainforest.

Singapore's only protected wetland, the Sungei Buloh Wetland Reserve (▷ 69), is home to over 500 species of tropical flora and fauna.

Cruise on a wooden bumboat to Pulau Ubin island (▷ 96–97), where you can explore mangrove swamps and cycle through tropical forests.

THRILL SEEKING

At Clarke Quay (▷ 29), get your heart pumping with a high-adrenaline G-Max Reverse Bungee or GX-5 rides.

Buzz down the 700yd (640m) Skyline Luge toboggan run, ride a wave at Wave House or try indoor skydiving at Sentosa (▷ 64–65).

BIRDS AND ANIMALS

At Jurong Bird Park (▷ 60–61), you can see around 400 species in walk-through aviaries.

Catch exotic nocturnal animals when they're active on a Night Safari (▷ 62–63).

Singapore Zoo (▷ 70–71) is the home of nearly 3,000 animals.

From top: view from 1-Altitude; Bukit Timah; Sentosa Mega Zip; Jurong Bird Park

Singapore by Area

The City

Immerse yourself in the galleries of world-class museums, stroll the vibrant streets and back lanes of Chinatown, or take a walk down Orchard Road.

2

3

Shrewsbury Road

CENTRAL EXPRESSWAY (CTE)

United Square

Hon Clan Temple

KAMPONG JAVA FLYOVER

KENG LEE ROAD

KAMPONG JAVA

Newton Circus

Newton

KAMPONG JAVA

BUKIT TIMAH

Swimming Complex

Farrer Field

Sri Veeramakaliamman Temple

LITTLE INDIA

4

American Club

Shaw Centre

Orchard

ION Orchard Mall

Orchard Road

Al-Falah Mosque

The Heeren

Ngee Ann City

Mandarin Arcade

Faber House

Starhub Centre

Centrepoint

Istana Presidential Palace

Free Church of Singapore

Istana Park

Sri Temasek

CITY

Mount Emily Park

Academy of Fine Arts

Church of Christ of Malaya

Peace Centre

The Verge

Bencoolen Mosque

5

GRANGE ROAD

Orchard Cineleisure

Somerset

Comcentre

EXETER RD EBER ROAD

House of Tan Yeok Nee

Chesed-El Synagogue

Church of the Sacred Heart

Sri Thendayuthapani Temple (Chettiar's Temple)

Singapore Buddhist Lodge

RIVER VALLEY ROAD

Dhoby Ghaut

Park Mall

Presbyterian Church

Maghain Aboth Synagogue

Singapore Art Museum

National Museum of Singapore

Fort Canning Park

Asian Sculpture Garden

National Archives

St Gregory's Armenian Church

Bras Basah

Cathedral of the Good Shepherd

Peranakan Museum

Funan IT Mall

Supreme Court

Parliament

6

KIM SENG BRIDGE

Singapore BRIDGE

Martin Road

CLEMENCEAU BRIDGE

Fort Canning Service Reservoir

Fort Canning

Clarke Quay

Singapore River Cruise

Melaka Mosque

Tan Si Chong Su Temple

Manhattan House

Havelock Square

HAVELOCK ROAD

READ BRIDGE

Clarke Quay

Riverwalk Galleria

COLEMAN BRIDGE

ELGIN BRIDGE

High Street Centre

Asian Civilisation Museum

Yueh Hai Ching Temple

Singapore River Cru

7

Pearl's Hill City Park

Pearl's Hill Reservoir

OUTRAM FLYOVER

People's Park Centre

People's Park Complex

Chinatown Complex Food Centre

Pearl Bank Apartment

Singapore General Hospital

Pearl's Centre

Outram Park

People's Theatre

Kreta Ayer

Oriental Plaza

Chinatown Point

Chinatown

CHINATOWN

Jamae Mosque

Sri Mariamman Temple

Nagore Durgha

Buddha Tooth Relic Temple and Museum

Thian Hock

Keng Temple

Fuk Tak Chi Museum

Telok Ayer

City House

Lau Pa Sa

St Matthew's Church

NEIL ROAD

Phoo Thor Chi Temple

Wallich Street

Tanjong Pagar

Seng Wong Beo Temple

Realty Centre

Anson Centre

Hock Teck See Temple

Temasek Tower

Singapore Conference Hall

GOLDEN BRIDGE

0   250 m
0   250 yds

8

C   **D**   **E**

BALESTIER ROAD

7C

RANGOON ROAD

OWEN ROAD

Farrer Park

Angullia Mosque

Little India Arcade

Rocher

Sim Lim Square

BENCOOLEN STREET

MIDDLE ROAD

BRAS BASAH ROAD

VICTORIA ST

ROAD

BEDEMEER RD

LAVENDER STREET

Tamil Malar

Sakaya Muni Buddha Gaya Temple

Sri Sivan Temple

Sri Srinivasa Perumal Temple

Serangoon Plaza

Mustafa Centre

Museum of Shanghai Toys

KITCHENER ROAD

JALAN BESAR

SYED

Abdul Gaffoor Mosque

Rochor Centre

ROCHOR CANAL ROAD

VICTORIA STREET

Bugis Junction

Bugis

BEACH RD

Bendemeer

KALLANG BAHRU

Jln Besar Stadium

SYED ALWI BRIDGE

Lavender

CRAWFORD STREET

VICTORIA BRIDGE

CRAWFORD BRIDGE

Old Malay Cemetery

Muslim Cemetery

KAMPONG GLAM

Sultan Mosque

Sultan Plaza

Golden Mile Complex

Arab Street

JALAN SULTAN ROAD

BEACH ROAD

KALLANG ROAD

Sri Manmathan Temple

NICOLL HIGHWAY

MERDEKA BRIDGE

Textile Centre/ Plaza Cinema

Bugis Street

St Joseph's Church

National Library

SS Peter & Paul

MINT Museum of Toys

Raffles Hotel

Chijmes

Raffles City

City Hall

St Andrew's Cathedral

The Padang

National Gallery Singapore

Victoria Concert Hall & Theatre

Lim Bo Seng Memorial

Cenotaph

Esplanade Theatres on the Bay

Outdoor Theatre

ESPLANADE BRIDGE

Jubilee Bridge

Merlion Park

Suntec City Mall

Fountain of Wealth

Singapore International Convention and Exhibition Centre

Esplanade

Millenia Walk

Promenade

War Memorial Park

Marina Square

RAFFLES BOULEVARD

NICOLL HIGHWAY

REPUBLIC AVENUE

Nicoll Highway

REPUBLIC BOULEVARD

BRIDGE

15

SHEARES

RAFFLES AVENUE

The Float @Marina Bay

The Helix Bridge

ArtScience Museum

Bayfront Bridge

BENJAMIN SHEARES AVENUE

Singapore Flyer

Marina Promenade Park

Marina Reservoir

Marina Promenade

Marina

The Fullerton Pavilion

BATTERY RD

FULLERTON ROAD

COLLYER QUAY

Raffles Place

Clifford Pier

The Promontory @Marina Bay

One Raffles Quay

Downtown

Central Boulevard

RAFFLES QUAY

Marina Bay Sands

Marina Bay

Expo and Convention Centre

Bayfront

red dot design museum

Flower Dome

Visitor Centre

Cloud Forest

Marina South Promenade

BAYFRONT AVENUE

SHEARES AVENUE

Gardens by the Bay (Bay South Gardens)

Marina Gardens Drive

Marina Mall

Marina Grove

Marina Barrage

Sustainable Singapore Gallery

MARINA COASTAL EXPRESSWAY (MCE)

Marina Boulevard

Marina Central Boulevard

Marina Bay

Straits Boulevard

Marina South

MARINA COASTAL EXPRESSWAY (MCE)

Marina Wharf

2

Marina South Pier

Singapore Maritime Gallery

Marina South Pier

3

F   G   H

Asian Civilisations Museum

HIGHLIGHTS

- Chinese history timeline
- Red bat motifs
- Buddhist statues
- Literati gallery
- Jade collection
- Qing Dynasty porcelain
- Kang tables
- Islamic collection

TIP

● Guided tours, given several times a day, are the perfect way to learn more about Asian culture.

Displaying relics of mainland China, continental India, Islamic West Asia and Southeast Asian cultures, this excellent museum is housed in a gorgeous colonial waterfront building.

Scene setter The imposing 1865 Empress Place building sets the stage for a fascinating look at the artistic, cultural and religious developments of Asia. Look for special exhibitions, lectures and seasonal festivals that illuminate the distinct Asian cultures covered exhaustively in this sprawling space.

Multimedia There are six themed galleries spread over three levels, each displaying artifacts that help paint a picture of these ancient Asian civilizations. The story of Asia's roots and

Clockwise from far left: a sandstone figure of Buddha (Cambodia, 11th–12th century); Lakhoun Khaol dance mask, also from Cambodia; a Chinese porcelain Buddha; a Kraak dish showing two Persian ladies of the Safavid period

evolution is revealed with fascinating displays, interactive exhibits and excellent multimedia presentations to help provide historical background for each of these disparate cultures.

The Singapore River Gallery tells of Chinese "coolies," of indigenous Orang Laut from Malaya and the more recently arrived Europeans. The West Asia Gallery explains the importance of the mosque in Islamic societies. The Southeast Asia Gallery is full of lavish textile exhibits, while the China Gallery has a fascinating "interview with the Emperor" video display, and a stunning life-size example of the Son of Heaven's yellow ceremonial robe.

To make the most of your visit, download ACM's app before you start. It includes a self-guided tour that provides stories and background on noteworthy exhibits.

THE BASICS

acm.org.sg

✚ F6

✉ 1 Empress Place

☎ 6332 7798

🕐 Daily 10–7 (Fri until 9)

🍴 Privé ACM; Empress

🚇 Raffles Place

🚌 75, 100, 130, 131, 167

♿ Good

✋ Moderate

❓ Free guided tours daily from 11am. Museum shops. Temporary exhibitions

Buddha Tooth Relic Temple and Museum

One of the pavilions in the rooftop garden (left); the magnificent gold stupa housing the sacred tooth (right)

THE BASICS

btrts.org.sg

☩ E7

✉ 288 South Bridge Road

☎ 6220 0220

🕐 Daily 7–7

🍴 Five Sights Hall serves simple vegetarian food (donation)

🚇 Chinatown

🚌 80, 145

♿ Moderate

✋ Free

HIGHLIGHTS

● Sacred Light Hall
● Evening closing ceremony
● Tang-style facade
● Rooftop pagoda
● Buddhist Culture Museum

TIP

● If you're craving more than vegetarian food, head to the adjacent Chinatown Food Street (▷ 52) or Chinatown Complex (▷ 28) for an abundance of local food options.

Singapore's most sacred Chinese Buddhist site, this striking Chinatown temple houses what practitioners believe is the left canine tooth of Buddha. Make time to admire the impressive Tang architecture and to see the other relics, too.

Tang-style temple Completed in 2007, the five-story temple was conceived by Chief Abbot Venerable Shi Fa Zhao, whose dramatic design was inspired by the traditional structures erected during China's Tang Dynasty (AD618–907). Inside, the first stop for most visitors is the fourth-floor Sacred Light Hall. This is where the Buddha Tooth Relic, purportedly uncovered in a fallen stupa in Myanmar, is stored in a massive stupa fashioned from 705lb (320kg) of donated gold. The rooftop terrace might be the most peaceful place in the temple, with four separate pavilions, a pretty orchid garden and the Ten Thousand Buddhas Pagoda, filled with gilded Buddha and Bodhisattva statues. It's a lovely spot to stop and linger, particularly in the morning and early evening, before the Mountain Gate closing ceremony. The temple, with all its red paintwork, looks breathtaking when floodlit after dark.

Museums Back downstairs, the atmospheric third-floor Buddhist Culture Museum has a number of other holy Buddhist relics and is an excellent place to learn more about the religion. The Eminent Sangha Museum on the mezzanine explores the lives of eminent monks.

Chinatown

The best time to visit Chinatown is just before Chinese New Year, when the streets throb and busy vendors sell everything from waxed ducks and steamed buns to *hong bao*, red packets for giving money as presents.

Conservation This area covers the streets leading off South Bridge Road between Maxwell Road and the Singapore River. As a policy, conservation of the old buildings goes hand-in-hand with new development here. Though better than destruction, the often rather cosmetic results and years of unsympathetic infilling have left only a few streets with the atmosphere and activities of old Chinatown.

What to see Erskine Road and Ann Siang Hill exhibit some of the best efforts of preservation. Temple and Trengganu streets (▷ 50) have many traditional shophouses and coffee shops, while Pagoda Street, similar in character, also has the Chinatown Heritage Centre. Nearby Smith Street is the area's appointed food alley, with lots of covered outdoor eating options. South Bridge Road, between Upper Cross Street and Maxwell Road, is home to fascinating places of worship. Telok Ayer Street, although much renovated, is also worth a visit. Thian Hock Keng Temple (the Temple of Heavenly Happiness) is the oldest Chinese temple in the city, while the newest addition is Buddha Tooth Relic Temple and Museum, farther along South Bridge Road (▷ 26).

THE BASICS

🚇 E7

✉ South Bridge Road and surrounding streets

🍴 Smith Street

🚇 Chinatown

🚌 2, 5, 12, 33, 51, 61, 62, 63, 81, 84, 103, 104, 124, 143, 145, 147, 166, 174, 181, 190, 197, 520, 851

♿ None

🎫 Free

HIGHLIGHTS

● Maxwell Road Food Centre
● Ann Siang Hill
● Chinese shophouses
● Buddha Tooth Relic Temple and Museum
● Chinatown Heritage Centre
● Chinatown Complex Food Centre (▷ 28)

TIP

● Come hungry—this is one of the best areas in Singapore for walking and snacking.

Chinatown Complex Food Centre

TOP 25

Spoilt for choice (left); the Hong Kong Soya Sauce Chicken Rice and Noodle (right)

THE BASICS

nea.gov.sg

🕂 E7

✉ 335 Smith Street

🕐 11–11

🚇 Chinatown

♿ Good

✋ Inexpensive

HIGHLIGHTS

● Hong Kong Soya Sauce
Chicken Rice and Noodle
● Smith Street Taps
● Claypot rice
● Zhong Guo La Mian Xiao
Long Bao
● 168 CMY Satay

TIP

● If you find yourself
overwhelmed by choice, a
good rule of thumb is to
look for a long line and join
it. The wait will probably
be worth it, though make
sure you know what you're
getting into since many
hawkers serve just one or
two dishes.

In one of the world's great food destinations it is the hawker centers—ubiquitous open-air food courts—that best showcase Singapore's endless culinary bounty. This hawker, in Chinatown, is one of the best.

Licensing street food Singapore's hawker centers were born in the 1950s, when government authorities began moving the city's street food vendors, many of them unlicensed, into new structures filled with stalls the vendors could lease at a subsidized rate and facilities to improve hygiene and cleanliness. Today there are more than 100 official hawker centers across the island and countless other similar, privately managed food courts. No matter the location, it's the food that counts—and Chinatown Complex scores points both for its wonderfully scruffy ambience and its cuisine.

Hawker feasts Every Singaporean has their own personal favorite hawker stalls and overall hawker centers, but few locals can dispute Chinatown Complex's culinary acumen. One of the oldest of its kind, this gargantuan hawker houses more than 200 vendors specializing in everything from roasted duck to claypot rice and Singaporean laksa. Most notable, perhaps, is Hong Kong Soya Sauce Chicken Rice and Noodle, the world's cheapest Michelin-starred restaurant. Other Michelin-listed stalls are 168 CMY Satay and Zhong Guo La Mian Xiao Long Bao. This is also where you'll find the craft beer hawkers at hidden Smith Street Taps (▷ 51).

Clarke Quay at dusk (left); chefs preparing food in a Clarke Quay restaurant (right)

Clarke Quay

The range of nightlife venues has grown so large in Singapore that it's difficult to pick the best. Nonetheless, for its scenic—and central—location, Clarke Quay is tough to beat.

Working quay Just upriver from the marina and the Raffles landing site, Clarke Quay, named after Singapore's second governor, Sir Andrew Clarke, was at the heart of the 19th-century trade route through Singapore.

Revival These days the whole quay area is owned by one of Asia's biggest real estate companies, who gave it a multimillion-dollar facelift. Five art deco godowns (blocks of warehouses) have been refurbished in pastel hues and covered with a climate-control canopy. Smaller lampshade covers line the riverfront and make it possible to sit out by the water without being bothered by the heat. There are more than 60 eating, entertainment, drinking, retail and lifestyle outlets, including buzzy Peranakan restaurant Violet Oon Satay Bar & Grill (▷ 54) and Motorino for New York-style pizza. It's a must-visit for tourists, but part of the attraction is that it's a party spot also loved by locals.

Thrill rides Clarke Quay is home to a pair of adrenaline-pumping rides—the G-Max Reverse Bungee and GX-5 Extreme Swing. The former pings riders skyward, while the other is a giant swing that arcs out across the Singapore River at speeds up to 75mph (120kph).

THE BASICS

clarkequay.com.sg
E6
3 River Valley Road
6337 3292
24 hours
Various
Clarke Quay
Generally good
Individual venues may charge a cover

HIGHLIGHTS

● Motorino Pizzeria
● Ramen Keisuke Lobster King
● The Pump Room
● Violet Oon Satay Bar & Grill
● Zouk

TIP

● Take advantage of the weekday happy hours offered at just about every Clarke Quay bar and restaurant from around 5pm.

Gardens by the Bay

HIGHLIGHTS

- Flower Dome
- Cloud Forest
- Supertree Grove
- Heritage Gardens
- The Meadow

Just a short walk from the Central Business District, this 250-acre (100-hectare) complex—split into three waterfront spaces—brings even more greenery to the already lush and tropical city.

Bay South Here you will find the Supertree Grove, arguably the park's top attraction. The 16-story-tall vertical gardens have been designed to collect rainwater, generate solar power and act as venting ducts for the park's conservatories. Make time for a walk along the OCBC Skyway, an elevated walkway linking two Supertrees—this is one of the best spots to take in the park's sweeping scenery. Nearby is The Meadow, Singapore's largest outdoor garden venue and a popular venue for big events and outdoor concerts.

THE CITY TOP 25

Hothouses Tropical trees and blossoms set the scene for a great evening stroll along the waterfront promenade, or beat the heat with a trip inside one of the two armadillo-shaped conservatories. The Cloud Forest has the world's largest indoor waterfall, while the Flower Dome houses plants from the Mediterranean and semi-arid subtropical regions.

Dining in the park A variety of top dining options are available at Gardens by the Bay. Pollen, located in the Flower Dome and helmed by executive chef Steve Allen, offers Mediterranean-influenced, modern European cuisine. If you prefer a more casual setting, try Satay by the Bay, or head to the top of the tallest Supertree for cocktails and Asian-Western fusion at the swish Indochine bistro.

THE BASICS

gardensbythebay.com.sg

✚ G7

✉ 18 Marina Gardens Drive

☎ 6420 6848

🕐 Outdoor gardens daily 5am–2am; conservatories and OCBC Skyway daily 9–9

🍴 Various

🚇 Bayfront

♿ Generally good

✋ Conservatories expensive; outdoor gardens free

Kampong Glam

Sultan Mosque (left); eateries on Beach Road (middle); pashminas on sale (right)

THE BASICS

Sultan Mosque
sultanmosque.sg
⊞ G4
✉ 3 Muscat Street
☎ 6293 4405
🕐 Sat–Thu 10–12, 2–4, Fri 2.30–4
🍴 Numerous coffee shops
Ⓜ Bugis
🚌 2, 32, 51, 61, 63, 84, 133, 145, 197
♿ None
👆 Free

HIGHLIGHTS

● Bussorah Street
● Sultan Mosque
● Prayer hall
● Istana Kampong Glam
● Murtabak
● Haji Lane
● Malay Heritage Centre

The golden domes and minarets of Sultan Mosque, glinting in the late-afternoon sun, and the call of the *muezzin* remind you that this area of Singapore is very much part of the Islamic world.

In the past Kampong Glam, where the Sultan of Singapore once lived, was set aside in the early days for Malay, Arab and Bugis (Sulawesi) traders. The "Glam" may derive from the *gelam* tree, from which medicinal oil was produced.

Today Although there are many mosques on the island, Sultan Mosque is the focus of worship for Singapore's Muslim (mainly Malay) community. There has been a mosque on this site since 1824, when the East India Company made a grant for its construction. The present mosque dates from 1928, and reveals an interesting mix of Middle Eastern and Moorish influences. Its gilded dome is impressive; unusually, its base is made from bottles. Seen as you walk up Bussorah Street, with its shophouses at the rear, the mosque is stunning. Visitors are welcome outside prayer times, as long as they are well covered—no shorts. The *istana* (palace), built in the 1840s, is at the top of Sultan Gate and houses the Malay Heritage Centre. The surrounding streets are filled with a mix of shops selling souk items like basketware, perfume and carpets, and independent boutiques offering the latest fashions. At night, the area's coffee shops, shisha cafés, cocktail bars and music lounges come alive.

Sri Veeramakaliamman Temple (left); the Mustafa Centre mall is open 24 hours (right)

Little India

There's never a dull moment in Little India. Along Serangoon Road and the surrounding streets you can experience an authentic microcosm of the sounds, scents and sensations of India.

Origins of Little India In the mid-19th century, lime pits and brick kilns were set up in the area, and it is thought that these attracted Singapore's Indians, who were laborers for the most part, to Serangoon Road. The swampy grasslands here were also good for raising cattle, another traditional occupation of the Indian community.

Little India today Rhythmic *tala* music fills the air, cluttered shops are packed with colorful garments and fresh flowers, and everywhere there's food, food and more food. The district remains overwhelmingly Indian, full of sari-clad women, spice shops, jasmine-garland sellers, Hindu temples and restaurants. Apart from the lively streets and vintage architecture, one notable highlight is Tekka Centre at the southern end of Serangoon Road, which has an excellent food center on the ground floor and clothes shops above. Across from the market, a little way up Serangoon Road, Komala Vilas restaurant (▷ 53) serves wonderful *dosai* (savory pancakes) and vegetarian curries. Walk along Serangoon Road and you will come to Sri Veeramakaliamman Temple, dedicated to the ferocious goddess Kali. Farther on still is the Sri Srinivasa Perumal Temple, noted for its magnificent 1979 *gopuram* (ornamental gateway).

THE BASICS

littleindia.com.sg
🔲 F4
✉ Serangoon Road
🍴 Many restaurants and cafés
🚇 Little India, Farrer Park
🚌 8, 13, 20, 23, 26, 31, 64, 65, 66, 67, 81, 90, 97, 103, 106, 111, 125, 131, 133, 139, 142, 147, 151, 154, 865
🎟 Free

HIGHLIGHTS

● Mustafa Centre (▷ 49)
● Banana-leaf meals
● Fish head curry
● Perfumed garlands
● Fortune-tellers
● Temples
● Spice shops

TIP

● The district heaves on Sundays, when throngs of guest workers (predominantly men) hit the streets on their one weekly day off.

Marina Bay Sands

TOP 25

Marina Bay Sands' three hotel towers are each 55 stories high

THE BASICS

marinabaysands.com

⊞ G7

✉ 10 Bayfront Avenue

☎ 6688 8868

🕙 Shoppes mall daily 10.30–11 (Fri–Sat till 11.30) but varies between shops; ArtScience Museum daily 10–7

🍴 Various

🚇 Bayfront

♿ ArtScience Museum good

💲 ArtScience Museum expensive

HIGHLIGHTS

● Celebrity restaurants
● Casino
● ArtScience Museum
● SkyPark
● The Shoppes at Marina Bay Sands

Resembling a surfboard sitting atop three high-rise buildings, this integrated resort is an iconic part of the Singapore skyline.

Architectural masterpiece The shape of a deck of cards inspired Israeli architect Moshe Safdie's blueprints for Marina Bay Sands, which includes the three main towers, the lotus-shaped ArtScience Museum and The Shoppes at Marina Bay Sands mall.

View from above Sands SkyPark on the 57th floor offers a 360-degree view of the skyline. Here you will find Sky on 57 restaurant and CÉ LA VI bar, and guests of Marina Bay Sands hotel can take a dip in the infinity pool.

ArtScience Museum This striking structure is incorporated into a laser light show every night, but the star attractions are inside. The 21 galleries celebrate creativity in all fields and have hosted a range of high-profile art and design exhibitions. The high-tech digital installation FutureWorld offers an immersive, interactive experience unlike anything you've tried before.

Inside the mall In addition to hosting more than 300 stores, including big-name brands like Prada and Louis Vuitton, the Shoppes at Marina Bay Sands complex is home to several celebrity chefs, including Gordon Ramsay (Bread Street Kitchen, ▷ 52). Here you'll also find a massive casino, two state-of-the-art performance theaters and an indoor canal.

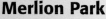
The iconic Merlion was created by the Singapore Tourism Board as city mascot in 1964

Merlion Park

Anchored around the water-spewing statue that has become Singapore's de facto mascot, Merlion Park is a prime spot to bask in the modern architectural glory that engulfs the downtown core.

Mythical mascot Crafted by Singaporean sculptor Lim Nang Seng, the Merlion statue is an 28ft-tall (8.5m) statue with a lion's head and a fish's body. The head nods to Singapore's traditional name, Singapura ("Lion City" in Sanskrit), while the body pays homage to the island's roots as a sleepy fishing village. Printed on every souvenir imaginable, the Merlion is easily Singapore's most marketed emblem.

Splendid scenery The Merlion may be the park's most prominent tenant, but even it can get lost among the structural splendors surrounding it on Marina Bay. The park is situated square in the middle of it all, with the Singapore Flyer Ferris wheel (▷ 42), lotus-shaped ArtScience Museum and three-towered Marina Bay Sands hotel (▷ 34) straight ahead, and the towering skyscrapers of the Central Business District to the left and right.

Exploring Hop aboard one of Singapore River Cruise's (▷ 46) wooden bumboats for a relaxing 40-minute spin around Marina Bay and down the Singapore River. Alternatively, the park is a good start or end point for a scenic walk along the river, which from Marina Bay stretches about 8 miles (5km) inland to Tanglin Road.

THE BASICS

visitsingapore.com
🕂 F6
✉ 1 Fullerton
🚇 Esplanade, Raffles Place
🚌 10, 57, 70, 75, 100
♿ Good
✋ Free

HIGHLIGHTS

● Merlion and Merlion Cub statues
● Marina Bay views
● Singapore River walk
● Laser light show
● Photo ops

TIP

● Make your way to the Merlion by 8 or 9pm (and 10pm Fri and Sat) for a prime vantage point of Marina Bay Sands' nightly 15-minute lights and water show.

THE CITY TOP 25

National Gallery Singapore

Part of the old Supreme Court building (right); the modern art gallery (left)

THE BASICS

nationalgallery.sg

➕ F6

✉ 1 St. Andrew's Road

☎ 6271 7000

🕐 Sat–Thu 10–7, Fri 10–9

🍽 Cafés, restaurant

🚇 City Hall

♿ Good

💰 Moderate

HIGHLIGHTS

● Singaporean art collection
● Southeast Asian art exhibitions
● Gallery Explorer app tours
● National Kitchen by Violet Oon
● Odette
● Aura Sky Lounge

TIP

● Splurge on the savory, spicy chili crab at National Kitchen. Oon's version is based on an old family recipe.

Taking over what used to be Singapore's Supreme Court building, the imposing National Gallery boasts the world's largest public collection of Southeast Asian and Singaporean art—and fantastic restaurants, too.

National treasure It isn't easy to stand out in increasingly arts-focused Singapore. Still, with its much-anticipated arrival in 2015, the National Gallery vaulted to the top of the ranks with its well-curated collection of more than 8,000 modern artworks from both local and regional artists. It's all spread out across two permanent galleries and a number of spaces used for temporary exhibitions. Highlights include the "Siapa Nama Kamu?" ("What is Your Name?") exhibition, an exceptional survey of Singapore's art history since the 19th century, and "Between Declarations and Dreams," a spotlight of Southeast Asian artists. Loaned artworks by Western artists are also displayed periodically.

Dinner and drinks The art isn't the only attraction at the National Gallery. At National Kitchen by Violet Oon (▷ 54), Singaporean food celebrity Violet Oon serves exceptional Nonya cuisine, a regional food style that draws from Chinese, Indonesian and Malayan cooking. Similarly upscale, Odette is a Michelin two-starred modern French restaurant that is consistently ranked among Asia's best eateries. Wrap up your evening with a cocktail under the stars at the rooftop Aura Sky Lounge.

The museum is housed in a colonial building (left); exhibits in the film gallery (right)

National Museum of Singapore

Originally opened as the Raffles Museum and Library in 1887, this palatial structure has been transformed into one of Singapore's most compelling museums.

Exploring the past The museum brings Singapore's rich history to life in 11 permanent exhibitions, complemented by a rotating series of temporary galleries. Don't miss the natural history drawings in the Goh Seng Choo Gallery of William Farquhar, Singapore's first British colonialist resident.

History and culture Singapore's documented history may be brief, but it's hardly short on intrigue. Precolonial history is dispensed within a single gallery, which includes the Singapore Stone, a lump of 1,000-year-old rock inscribed with a language that has never been deciphered. The Crown Colony gallery explores life in the city between Stamford Raffles' arrival in 1819 and World War II, while the Syonan-To exhibit uses many personal artifacts to tell the story of life under Japanese occupation. The modern Singapore gallery carries the story up through independence to the present day. The optional audio guide significantly enhances the overall experience with extra information, commentaries and dramatizations. The lifestyle galleries are very interactive and feature pared-down exhibitions on food, photography, fashion and film. Gallery10 has no physical artifacts on display at all but projects viewers via video into a dance rehearsal in the backstreets.

THE BASICS

nationalmuseum.sg
✚ E5
✉ 93 Stamford Road
☎ 6332 3659
🕐 Daily 10–7 (last entry 6.30)
🍴 Fine-dining restaurants and an all-day café
🚇 Bras Basah, Dhoby Ghaut
🚍 Many, including 7, 14, 16 and 36
♿ Good
💰 Moderate
❓ Free English-language tours of the history gallery on some days. National Museum app

HIGHLIGHTS

● Singapore History Gallery
● The Singapore Stone
● Personal testimony from POWs interned by Japan
● Exhibition of Asia's herbs and spices in the Food Gallery

THE CITY TOP 25

Orchard Road

- Food courts
- Paragon
- Books Kinokuniya
- Takashimaya
- ION Sky
- Orchard Central
- Mandarin Gallery

TIP

- Time your visit for the early evening hours, when the deafening sound of thousands of chirping birds perched in trees along Orchard Road fills the air.

Orchard Road is the retail heart and soul of Singapore, and one of Asia's glitziest shopping boulevards. Day or night, a stroll from one end to the other is a pleasure, even if you don't shop.

Room to move Wide sidewalks and snacks aplenty help make the cosmopolitan charms of Orchard Road a pleasure. And escaping the extreme heat that this equatorial city experiences is as easy as dashing into one of the dozens of air-conditioned shopping malls that line the street. Goods from all parts of the world are on offer, including electrical items, designer fashions, antiques and gifts. Inexpensive food courts are prevalent and there are any number of good restaurants. For a good walking tour, start at Centrepoint, near Somerset Station, and

Clockwise from left: ION Orchard mall is the area's flagship mall; Mandarin Gallery; the bustle doesn't die down after dark

walk to Tanglin Mall at the western end of the street. On the way, pause near the intersection with Scotts Road to drop in at ION Orchard, or take in a film at the nearby Lido Cineplex.

Mall heaven While the first malls appeared along this shopping drag in the 1970s, it's been non-stop development ever since, with the latest major revamp in 2009. This was when ION Orchard was added, with its curvaceous futuristic design, 300-plus shops and sweeping 56th-floor observation desk, ION Sky. Orchard Central, which is the same age, is Singapore's tallest mall, with 14 floors of retail space, including two below ground level. The four-level Mandarin Gallery is another retail haven, hosting such top international brands as Victoria's Secret and Michael Kors.

THE BASICS

orchardroad.org

C4/D5/E5

Restaurants, food courts, supermarkets

Orchard, Somerset

7, 14, 16, 65, 106, 111, 123, 167, 605

Good

Raffles Hotel

Raffles Hotel exterior (left); the elegant Raffles Courtyard at the back of the main building (right)

THE CITY TOP 25

THE BASICS

rafflessingapore.com

✚ F5

✉ 1 Beach Road

☎ 6337 1886

🍴 Tiffin Room, afternoon tea, heritage bars, cafés and restaurants

🚇 City Hall

🚌 14, 16, 36, 56, 82, 100, 107, 125, 167

♿ Good

HIGHLIGHTS

● Front facade
● Lobby
● Tiffin Room
● Bar and Billiard Room
● Singapore Sling
● Palm Court
● Long Bar

Even after a series of facelifts and renovations to this grand old dame of Singaporean luxury hotels, Raffles retains its colonial character and remains one of the world's truly great heritage hotels.

Legend Say "Raffles" and you conjure up an image of the very epitome of colonial style and service. Established by the Sarkies brothers in 1887, the hotel served the traders and travelers who, after the opening of the Suez Canal in 1869, were visiting the bustling commercial hub of Singapore in growing numbers. Over the years guests have included Somerset Maugham, Elizabeth Taylor, Noël Coward, Michael Jackson and Rudyard Kipling.

Renowned establishment Within just a decade of opening, the original 10-room bungalow had been expanded and the two-story wings added. The main building was opened in 1899. Over the years the Raffles Hotel has acquired a worldwide reputation for fine service and food, with its charming blend of classical architecture and tropical gardens. Sensitive restoration in 2018 aimed to preserve the hotel's colonial charm while fully updating its facilities.

Other facilities The Jubilee Hall is a charming Victorian-style theater that hosts all sorts of ceremonies and events throughout the year. Some 70 specialist shops adjoin the main building, including one dedicated to selling Raffles memorabilia.

Singapore Art Museum

This was Singapore's first art museum and is now dedicated to the collection and display of contemporary works from Singapore and Southeast Asia. It also hosts the prestigious Singapore Biennale.

National treasure The museum is housed in the restored 19th-century St. Joseph's Institution building, a former Catholic boys' school, and displays Singapore's national art collection. The permanent collection has grown from less than 2,000 artworks to more than 10,000, and now houses the largest and most comprehensive collection of 20th-century Southeast Asian art in the region, complemented by international works.

State of the art Almost 107,600sq ft (10,000sq m) of floor space includes 14 galleries, a reference library, an auditorium, a multipurpose hall, a museum shop, courtyards and an electronic E-image Gallery that runs interactive programs featuring some of the museum's collection on a large visual monitor. Check out Museum Label SAM at 8Q, a museum extension round the corner at 8 Queen Street, displaying a selection of multidisciplinary and interactive works.

On show An overview of Singaporean art is on permanent display and traveling exhibitions expose the region internationally. A community program covers a diversity of art trends and practices, fringe activities and lectures.

THE BASICS

singaporeartmuseum.sg
- F5
- 71 Bras Basah Road
- 6589 9580
- Daily 10–7 (Fri 10–9)
- Café adjacent
- Dhoby Ghaut, Bras Basah
- 14, 16, 36, 77, 124, 131, 162, 174
- Few
- Moderate; free admission Fri 6–9
- Free guided tours daily from 11. Museum shop

HIGHLIGHTS

- 19th-century building
- Large collection
- E-image Gallery
- Library
- Temporary exhibitions

Singapore Flyer

TOP 25

The observation wheel (left); view from one of the cabins (right)

THE BASICS

singaporeflyer.com.sg

✚ G6

✉ 30 Raffles Avenue

☎ 6734 8829

🕐 Daily 8.30am–10.30pm

🍴 Seafood, steak, Mexican, Japanese, among others

Ⓟ Promenade

♿ Good

💸 Expensive

❓ The security procedures are similar to an airport, and it's best to allow up to 30 min to collect tickets and pass through the checkpoints. For an extra S$40, you can enjoy a cocktail during your ride

HIGHLIGHTS

● Views ranging as far as Malaysia and Indonesia on clear days

● Singapore's sparkling nighttime skyline

One of the world's largest observation wheels, the Singapore Flyer offers a spectacular perspective on the urban heart of Singapore, with Malaysia and Indonesia also visible on clear days.

Orientation Perched on the edge of the Marina, and climbing to an impressive 541ft (165m), the Singapore Flyer is 100ft (30m) taller than the London Eye and a prominent feature on the skyline. The ever-changing perspective and pedestrian speed make it a great way to familiarize yourself with the layout of the Marina Bay Sands development below.

Panoramic views The ride lasts around 35 minutes and begins with views back across the Marina to the skyscrapers of the Central Business District. This angle also offers a great overview of the impressive Marina Bay Sands architecture (▷ 34). The downward section focuses attention on the north of the city, taking in Kampong Glam, Little India and the northeastern districts of Geylang and Katong.

The ride Each air-conditioned capsule accommodates up to 28 people. There are two screens in each capsule but, disappointingly, these broadcast commercials and funk music rather than any commentary on the landmarks (though you will be informed when you've reached the top of the ride). There's also a three-story, airport terminal-style building at the base of the wheel with shops and restaurants.

ARAB STREET

Vendors sell quality handicrafts from around Asia near the intersection of Beach Road and Arab Street, where some of the area's original shops still survive. Look for basketware, textiles (silks and batiks), lace, silverwork, jewelry and perfume. There are plenty of tempting restaurants, too.

➕ G4/5 ✉ Between North Bridge Road and Beach Road 🚇 Bugis

BUGIS STREET

Redeveloped in 1991 roughly 450ft (137m) from its original site, Bugis Street is divided into two sharply contrasting sections on either side of Victoria Street. The western stretch is most fun and contains the largest covered outdoor market in town. Expect plenty of fashion, crafts, curios and, of course, abundant food and drink options, including fresh fruit and veg stalls near Albert Street. Bugis Street east of Victoria Street is dominated by the Bugis Junction shopping plaza, a collection of brand-name shops and indie stores in air-conditioned surrounds that still manage to preserve the old shophouse facades.

➕ F5 ✉ Bugis Street 🕐 Outdoor market open daily until midnight. Bars open daily to 2 or 3am 🍴 Fast-food outlets 🚇 Bugis 🚌 2, 5, 7, 12, 32, 61, 62, 63, 84, 130, 160, 197, 520, 851, 960 ♿ Few (pedestrian precinct)

CHETTIAR'S TEMPLE

sttemple.com

The temple of Sri Thandayuthanapani, rebuilt in 1983, is also called Chettiar's Temple after the Indian *chettiars* (moneylenders) who financed its construction in the 1850s. Each glass panel of the unusual 48-panel ceiling frieze, from India, features a deity from the Hindu pantheon. The riotous *gopuram* was built five stories high so it could easily be seen from afar.

➕ E6 ✉ 15 Tank Road ☎ 6737 9393 🕐 Daily 8–12, 5.30–8.30 🚇 Dhoby Ghaut 🎫 Free

Outside Chettiar's Temple

Arab Street shop display

ESPLANADE—THEATRES ON THE BAY

esplanade.com

Nicknamed "the durians" for its shape—two glass domes covered with thousands of "prickles" (actually triangular aluminum sunshades)—this stunning waterfront theater and entertainment complex hosts a wide array of local and international performers in world-class facilities. The Concert Hall seats 1,600 and the Lyric Theatre 2,000, while the outdoor stage often offers free performances.

🚇 F6 ✉ 1 Esplanade Drive ☎ 6828 8377 🕐 Daily 10–10; 45-min tours Tue–Fri at 9, 12.30, 2, Sat–Sun at 9 🚇 Esplanade 🚻 Good 🎫 Tours moderate

FORT CANNING PARK

nparks.gov.sg

Spanning around 45 acres (18ha) of hilly, verdant green space slap bang in the middle of downtown, this gorgeous park is a perfect place to work up a sweat on a long morning or early evening hike. There's plenty of historical interest here, too, as the site of 14th-century palaces and the former headquarters of the British army. In fact, it was at Fort Canning Park in 1942 that Lieutenant-General Percival controversially decided to surrender to weaker Japanese forces during World War II. The underground bunker where that took place, today known as Battlebox, is open to the public and contains an exhibition on how the command center functioned during the war.

🚇 E5/6 ✉ River Valley Road ☎ 1800 471 7300 🍴 Two restaurants 🚇 Fort Canning, Clarke Quay or Dhoby Ghaut 🚻 Good 🎫 Park free; Battlebox moderate

HINDU TEMPLES

sttemple.com, smt.org.sg, sriveeramakaliamman.com

Around 5 percent of Singapore residents practice Hinduism, and three of the religion's most important temples here are well worth

Statue in the Sri Mariamman Temple

Mickey Mouse exhibit at the Mint Museum of Toys

visiting. Sri Mariamman Temple, a multicolored shrine with brilliant statuary on the tower, is located in Chinatown. It is the island's oldest Hindu temple, built in 1827, 30 years before Chettiar's Temple (▷ 43), the next oldest. Sri Veeramakaliamman Temple (▷ 33) was the first Hindu temple constructed in Little India. Each temple is open to the public, but these very much remain places of worship. Behave respectfully, and don't forget to remove your footwear before entering.

Sri Mariamman ➕ E7 ✉ 244 South Bridge Road ♿ Limited 🎫 Free
Sri Veeramakaliamman ➕ F4 ✉ 141 Serangoon Road ♿ Limited 🎫 Free

MINT MUSEUM OF TOYS
emint.com

This five-floor museum brings in toys from 25 countries, including some rare and valuable antiques up to a century old. The exhibitions will likely induce nostalgia among big kids and high excitement among adult collectors, though there's educational value for younger visitors with some hands-on displays. Mr. Punch restaurant (in the basement) and Winebar (on the roof) are both worth a visit. There are also collectables to buy, thematically linked to the toys in the main exhibition.

➕ F5 ✉ 26 Seah Street ☎ 6339 0660 🕐 Daily 9.30–6.30 🍴 Restaurant and bar 🚇 City Hall, Bugis ♿ Good 🎫 Moderate

THE PADANG

Once the Padang directly faced the sea, but land reclamation in Marina Bay has long since changed its outlook. This huge rectangular lawn—*padang* means "field" in Malay—which goes back to Raffles' days, has retained its use as a recreational area. Cricket and rugby matches are played in season and while non-members may not venture into the clubs, they can stand and watch the games. City Hall, facing the Padang, has seen several historic events: the herding of

Peranakan Museum (▷ 46)

Europeans onto the Padang on the morning of the Japanese occupation, and the formal surrender of the Japanese on its steps in 1945. At the southern end is the Cricket Club, the hub of colonial society in the 19th century, with a commanding view of the Padang. The group of government buildings includes the attorney-general's chambers (resembling a small opera house), the Victoria Theatre and Concert Hall buildings, and the former Parliament House.

➕ F6 ✉ 3 St. Andrew's Road 🚇 City Hall 🚌 10, 70, 75, 82, 97, 100, 107, 125, 130, 131, 167, 196 🚹 None 🖐 Free

PERANAKAN MUSEUM

peranakanmuseum.org.sg

This excellent museum documents Singapore's most fascinating minority race, the Peranakans. This slightly ambiguous term refers to descendants of mixed-race marriages between Malays and Chinese or Indian settlers. The displays here focus mainly on the Chinese Peranakan culture. The first floor is given over to Peranakan wedding rituals, with more focused exhibits on fashion, eating and religion on the second floor—and both give a fascinating insight into how the Peranakans, and Singaporeans, have learned to blend cultures. To better understand the meaning of "Peranakan," begin your visit by watching the "talking heads" video on the second floor.

➕ E5/6 ✉ 39 Armenian Street ☎ 6332 7591 🕐 Mon 1–6, Tue–Sun 9–7 (until 9pm Fri) 🍽 Restaurants and cafés nearby 🚇 Bras Basah 🚹 Good 🖐 Inexpensive. Free Fri 7–9

RED DOT DESIGN MUSEUM

museum.red-dot.sg

Conveniently located since 2017 in a striking, glass-fronted structure along Marina Bay, the museum presents a fascinating exhibition space that showcases winners of the prized international Red Dot Design Award. The displays are divided between imaginative design concepts yet to be given commercial backing, and finished products that have set the standard in their field, spanning everything from mechanized gadgetry to children's toys. On most weekends, the museum hosts MAAD market, a showcase for creative local designers and artists who set up stalls to hawk their work.

➕ E8 ✉ 11 Marina Boulevard ☎ 6514 0111 🕐 Mon–Thu 10–8, Fri–Sun 10am–11pm 🍽 Café and bar 🚇 Bayfront 🚹 Good 🖐 Moderate ❓ Occasionally closed for private events so call ahead

SINGAPORE RIVER CRUISE

rivercruise.com.sg

It's certainly a bit touristy, but cruising the Singapore River aboard a decorative wooden bumboat is nevertheless a fun way to take in downtown's modern architectural marvels. The Singapore River Cruise company operates from 13 jetties along the river, including at Clarke Quay and Merlion Park. The "Tale of 2 Quays" tour lasts about 40 minutes and loops around Marina Bay, while the twice-nightly laser cruise offers an aquatic perch from which to view the Marina Bay Sands hotel's laser light shows.

➕ E6 ✉ 30 Merchant Road, Clarke Quay ☎ 6336 6111 🖐 Expensive

Around Singapore's Historic Core

Get a feel for both the old and new Singapore with this long walk that includes temples and the grand Raffles Hotel.

DISTANCE: 5 miles (8km) **ALLOW:** 5 hours, including visits

START

MAXWELL ROAD
🔶 E7 🚇 Tanjong Pagar

1 From Maxwell Road walk down South Bridge Road to visit the Buddha Tooth Relic Temple (▷ 26). Turn left down South Street and return to South Bridge Road via Trengganu and Pagoda streets.

2 Note the renovated Chinese shophouses and visit the Sri Mariamman Temple (▷ 44–45). Cross over and take Ann Siang Hill, then turn left down Club Street.

3 Turn right at Cross Street and left into Telok Ayer Street. Far East Square and China Square are full of places to eat. Check out Fuk Tak Chi temple.

4 Turn right down Cheang Hong Lim Place and left at the end of Church Street and follow Market Street and Malacca Place to Raffles Place. Head north to reach Bonham Street and turn left into Boat Quay.

END

ARAB STREET
🔶 G4 🚇 Bugis

8 Wander around the streets lined with old shops selling cloth and handicrafts. Return to your hotel.

7 After Raffles City is Raffles Hotel (▷ 40). Continue along Beach Road. Turn left onto Arab Street, right onto Baghdad Street and left onto Bussorah Street. Facing Sultan Mosque (▷ 32), take the side street to your left, then head up Arab Street to Victoria Street.

6 Cross and pass Empress Place on the riverside promenade before turning right into Old Parliament Lane to pass the Victoria Concert Hall. On the right is Singapore Cricket Club. Cross over High Street and take St Andrew's Road. The Padang (▷ 45–46) is on your right.

5 Walk along the riverbank until you come to Cavenagh Bridge.

Shopping

313@SOMERSET

313somerset.com.sg

Set up above the Somerset MRT station, this eight-floor mall offers an eclectic mix of fashion brands. It's home to everything from Forever 21's Singapore flagship to a range of shops from contemporary European designers.

🚇 D5 ✉ 313 Orchard Road ☎ 6496 9313 🕐 Sun–Thu 10–10, Fri–Sat 10am–11pm 🚉 Somerset

CENTREPOINT

fraserscentrepointmalls.com

This is one of Singapore's most user-friendly complexes, with good department stores (Robinson's and Marks & Spencer) and shops selling everything from books to clothes and electrical goods, plus restaurants and a supermarket.

🚇 D5 ✉ 176 Orchard Road ☎ 6737 9000 🕐 Daily 10–10 🚉 Somerset

CHINATOWN POINT

One of Chinatown's earliest shopping centers, this mall contains a diverse variety of shops and eateries. Most notable, perhaps, is the number of vintage shops, with a particular focus on toys and comics.

🚇 E7 ✉ 133 New Bridge Road ☎ 6702 0114 🕐 Daily 10–10 🚉 Chinatown

ION ORCHARD

ionorchard.com

Architecturally stunning on the outside, the choice of more than 300 shops makes this modern mall equally awesome on the inside. Top brands like Louis Vuitton, Prada, Burberry and Dior can all be found within these futuristic walls.

🚇 C4 ✉ 2 Orchard Turn ☎ 6238 8228 🕐 Daily 10–10 🚉 Orchard

LUCKY PLAZA

luckyplazashopping.com

Another huge shopping complex on Orchard Road, Lucky Plaza is full of small shops selling all manner of goods. It's popular with local Indonesian and Philippine residents. Salespeople may be aggressive, so bargain hard.

🚇 D5 ✉ 304 Orchard Road ☎ 6235 3294 🕐 Daily 10–7 (but individual shop times vary) 🚉 Orchard

MANDARIN GALLERY

mandaringallery.com.sg

A sophisticated addition to the shopping strip, the gallery is home to quality labels such as Boss, Michael Kors and Bimba y Lola, along with luxury stationer's Elephant & Coral, which interestingly also stocks rare Japanese whiskies.

🚇 D5 ✉ 333 Orchard Road ☎ 6831 6363 🕐 Daily 11–9.30 🚉 Somerset

MATA HARI ANTIQUES

The basketry, lacquerware and silver jewelry here come from all over Southeast Asia.

🚇 E7 ✉ 13 Ann Siang Hill ☎ 6737 6068 🕐 Wed–Sun noon–8 🚉 Chinatown

MILLENIA WALK

milleniawalk.com

There are more than 190 designer and street-smart fashion stores and specialty

---

HONG BAO

You may notice small red packets on sale. These *hong bao*, as they are known, are used for giving gifts of money, particularly for weddings and at Chinese New Year, when it is the custom for unmarried children to receive a red packet. Many employers also choose this time of year to give their red packets—bonuses.

shops here, such as Hue, jewelers Hour Glass and Cortina E'space, and electrical superstore Harvey Norman.

🔀 G6 ✉ 9 Raffles Boulevard ☎ 6883 1122 🕐 Daily 10–10 🚇 City Hall

MUSTAFA CENTRE

mustafa.com.sg

More than 75,000 items fill four floors in Singapore's only 24-hour mall. Clothing, CDs, jewelry and cameras are just some of the items you can pick up here. Great for bargain-hunters.

🔀 F3 ✉ 145 Syed Alwi Road ☎ 6295 5855 🕐 24 hours, 7 days 🚇 Farrer Park

NGEE ANN CITY

ngeeanncity.com.sg

Anchored by Japanese department store Takashimaya, this mall has a nice mix of luxury (Chanel, Tiffany) and mid-range (Zara, Crabtree & Evelyn) brand-name stores, and it also has the city's largest bookstore, Kinokuniya.

🔀 D5 ✉ 391 Orchard Road ☎ 6506 0460 🕐 Daily 10–9.30 🚇 Somerset, Orchard

ORCHARD CENTRAL

orchardcentral.com.sg

Filled with shops catering to the rising hipster community of Singapore, cool fashion can be checked out in places like Audaash for women or Assemble for men. Beauty and wellness outlets like Haach add the finishing touches.

🔀 D5 ✉ 181 Orchard Road ☎ 6238 1051 🕐 Daily 11–10 🚇 Somerset

PARAGON

paragon.com.sg

One of the higher-end shopping malls along Orchard Road, Paragon has outlets for such well-known international fashion brands as Coach, Diesel, Ermenegildo Zegna and Jimmy Choo.

There are some great restaurants in the basement, too.

🔀 D5 ✉ 90 Orchard Road ☎ 6738 5535 🕐 Daily 10–10 🚇 Somerset

PEOPLE'S PARK COMPLEX

You can buy all manner of goods at this bustling complex in Chinatown, including Chinese medicines, Asian textiles, clothing and electronics.

🔀 E7 ✉ 1 Park Road ☎ 6535 9533 🕐 Daily 10–9.45 🚇 Outram Park

RAFFLES CITY

rafflescity.com.sg

The four-story mall section of this I.M. Pei-designed "city within a city" has floors dedicated to luxury buyers, fashionistas and children. It's one of Singapore's most accessible malls.

🔀 G4 ✉ 252 North Bridge Road ☎ 6338 7766 🕐 Daily 10–9.30 🚇 City Hall

SUNTEC CITY MALL

sunteccity.com.sg

Shoppers are welcomed by the Fountain of Wealth at one of Singapore's largest shopping malls. You'll find brand-name stores and specialty shops, including the G2000 flagship store and Mango.

🔀 G5 ✉ 3 Temasek Boulevard ☎ 6825 2667 🕐 Daily 10–10 🚇 Esplanade, Promenade

---

BARGAINING

Many Singapore shopkeepers are happy for you to bargain with them and it can save you a significant percentage, even on fairly small purchases. Don't make your first offer until the seller has reduced the opening price at least once. It is considered a matter of honor that once you have settled on a price, you must go through with the deal. Don't bargain if you see "Fixed price" signs.

TANGS

tangs.com

On the corner of Orchard and Scotts roads, you can't miss this popular department store, noted for its unique facade inspired by the Imperial Palace in Beijing's Forbidden City. You'll find a range of good-quality housewares, fashion, gifts and much more here.

🔒 C4 ✉ 320 Orchard Road ☎ 6737 5500
🕐 Mon–Thu 10.30–9.30, Fri–Sat 10.30am–11pm, Sun 11–8.30 🚇 Orchard

TEMPLE/PAGODA/ TRENGGANU STREETS

In the streets between South Bridge Road and New Bridge Road, in the heart of Chinatown, shops and stalls sell a tantalizing range of Chinese goods: herbal remedies, porcelain, exotic fruit and gold jewelry. The rich smell of barbecued pork pervades the streets.

🔒 E7 ✉ Off South Bridge Road
🚇 Chinatown

YUE HWA CHINESE PRODUCTS EMPORIUM

yuehwa.com.sg

This well laid-out Chinatown department store has an array of quality merchandise, from traditional clothes to handicrafts, jewelry, cosmetics and household items.

🔒 E7 ✉ 70 Eu Tong Sen Street ☎ 6538 4222 🕐 Sun–Fri 11–9, Sat 11–10
🚇 Chinatown

Entertainment and Nightlife

1-ALTITUDE

1-altitude.com

The highest rooftop bar in Singapore, 1-Altitude fills the top three floors in One Raffles Place: a sports bar on Level 61, European restaurant Stellar on 62 and alfresco bar with great views on 63.

🔒 F7 ✉ 1 Raffles Place ☎ 6438 0410
🕐 Mon–Thu 6pm–2am, Fri–Sat 6pm–4am, Sun 6pm–1am 🚇 Raffles Place

28 HONGKONG STREET

28hks.com

It's easy to wander past the entrance without noticing, as there is no signage outside. The cocktails are among the best and priciest in the city.

🔒 E6 ✉ 28 Hong Kong Street ☎ 6533 2001
🕐 Mon–Thu 5.30pm–1am, Fri–Sat 5.30pm–3am 🚇 Clarke Quay

BREWERKZ

brewerkz.com

Singapore's longest-running brewpub spills onto the banks of the Singapore River across from Clarke Quay. Five

---

WHAT'S ON

Concerts and theater are very popular, particularly for weekend shows. Details of events, their venues and where to buy tickets can be found in Singapore's daily morning newspaper, the *Straits Times,* and various free publications. Tickets for most major events are obtainable from SISTIC online, by phone or at outlets including Changi Airport, Esplanade—Theatres on the Bay, ION Orchard, Chinatown Point, Centrepoint, Wisma Atria, Raffles City Shopping Centre and Bugis Junction.

signature brews are on tap year round, plus seasonal and experimental beers and food staples like burgers and pizza.
🔢 E6 ✉ 30 Merchant Road, Riverside Point, #01-05 ☎ 6438 7438 🕐 Sun–Thu noon–midnight, Fri–Sat noon–1am 🚇 Clarke Quay

CÉ LA VI

sg.celavi.com
The bar/restaurant perched on top of Marina Bay Sands is modeled after one of the most popular hangouts in Bali. There are great views of the city, and entrance is free before 9pm.
🔢 G7 ✉ 1 Bayfront Avenue ☎ 6688 7688 🕐 Daily 11am–late 🚇 Bayfront

DRUGGISTS

Set on the first floor of a gorgeous shophouse still occupied (upstairs) by the Chinese Druggists Association, this laid-back craft beer venue pairs 23 taps with good vibes.
🔢 E6 ✉ 119 Tyrwhitt Road ☎ 6341 5967 🕐 Mon–Thu 4pm–midnight, Fri–Sat 4pm–2am, Sun 2–10 🚇 Lavender

GOOD LUCK BEERHOUSE

facebook.com/goodluckbeerhouse
This shoebox-sized craft beer bar on artsy Haji Lane has more than 50 bottles and cans in the fridge and, often, locally brewed Singaporean beer on the taps.
🔢 G4 ✉ 9 Haji Lane ☎ 8742 4809 🕐 Daily 12–12 🚇 Bugis

LEVEL33

level33.com.sg
Head 33 floors up to the "world's highest urban craft brewery" for house-brewed beers, upscale European cuisine and incredible views of downtown.
🔢 F6 ✉ 8 Marina Boulevard, Marina Bay Financial Centre Tower 1, #33-01 ☎ 6834

3133 🕐 Mon–Thu 11.30am–midnight, Fri–Sat 11.30am–2am, Sun 12–12 🚇 Raffles Place

MANHATTAN

regenthotels.com
Located in the Regent Singapore hotel, this swish cocktail bar is consistently rated one of the very best in Asia.
🔢 E5 ✉ 1 Cuscaden Road, Level 2 ☎ 6725 3377 🕐 Sun–Thu 5pm–1am, Fri–Sat 5pm–2am 🚇 Orchard

SMITH STREET TAPS

facebook.com/smithstreettaps
Tucked away on the second floor of Chinatown Complex Food Centre, this is Singapore's premier craft beer watering hole. Rare imports and the occasional local brew flow from the stall's 11 taps.
🔢 E5 ✉ Block 335 Smith Street, Chinatown Complex, #02-062 🕐 Tue–Fri 6.30am–10.30pm, Sat 2–10.30 🚇 Chinatown

ZOUK

zoukclub.com
Five different clubs make up Singapore's longest-running nightlife venue. Excellent in-house and guest DJs play the latest dance tracks.
🔢 D6 ✉ 17-21 Jiak Kim Street ☎ 6738 2988 🕐 Times vary 🚌 16, 75, 175

GRAB A DRINK

After working a 10- to 12-hour day, your average Singaporean either heads straight home or stops at a favorite bar en route. Weekends see increased nightlife activity; clubs do a roaring trade and attract expats and locals alike. As in other large cities, there is a good selection of Irish pubs and October brings German-inspired beer fests. And don't leave the city without having a Singapore Sling at the famous Long Bar at Raffles Hotel (▷ 40).

Where to Eat

THE BANANA LEAF APOLO ($$)

Proud holder of the world record for "most fish heads served at a single dinner" (2,012), this Little India mainstay serves reliably delicious Indian cuisine, with fish-head curry the signature dish. This place is usually packed.

➕ F4 ✉ 54 Race Course Road ☎ 6293 8682 ⏰ Daily 11–10.30 🚇 Little India

BENG THIN HOON KEE ($)

Hokkien food is popular in Singapore, for the ancestors of many Singaporeans lived in southern China, where the cuisine originated. Try the duck in lotus leaves.

➕ F7 ✉ 05–02 OCBC Building, 65 Chulia Street ☎ 6533 7708 ⏰ Daily 11.30–3, 6–10 🚇 Raffles Place

BLUE GINGER ($$)

theblueginger.com

Set in an old shophouse, this is the best place in Singapore to try Peranakan dishes such as fried pork and prawn rolls, *ayam panggang* (chicken in coconut milk) and durian desserts.

➕ E8 ✉ 97 Tanjong Pagar Road, Chinatown ☎ 6222 3928 ⏰ Daily 12–2.30, 6.30–10.30 🚇 Tanjong Pagar

BREAD STREET KITCHEN ($$$)

marinabaysands.com

International food superchef Gordon Ramsey exported this acclaimed London bistro to the sprawling Marina Bay Sands complex, home to a number of celebrity chef restaurants. Expect modern (and more expensive) British pub grub like roasted sea trout, sirloin steak and, of course, proper fish and chips.

➕ G7 ✉ 2 Bayfront Avenue, The Shoppes at Marina Bay Sands, #01-81 ☎ 6688 5665 ⏰ Mon–Thu 11.30am–1am, Fri 11.30am–2am, Sat 7.30am–2am, Sun 7.30am–1am 🚇 Bayfront 🚌 97, 106, 133

BURNT ENDS ($$$)

burntends.com.sg

Succulent Australian barbecue is the name of the game at this wildly popular smokehouse located just off Keong Saik Road, one of Singapore's liveliest food hubs.

➕ E7 ✉ 20 Teck Lim Road ☎ 6224 3933 ⏰ Tue–Thu 6pm–late, Fri–Sat 11.45–2, 6–late 🚇 Chinatown

CHINATOWN FOOD STREET ($)

chinatownfoodstreet.sg

This side street is lined with open-air stalls that come into their own after dark. Most types of local Chinese food are available plus bottled beer and a range of desserts—try the ice *kacang,* made of shaved ice and red beans with a choice of toppings.

➕ E7 ✉ Smith Street ⏰ Daily early–late 🚇 Chinatown

SATAY

No trip to Singapore would be complete without the famous satay, a Malay dish. Sticks of chicken, lamb or beef, and sometimes other foods such as tofu, are barbecued and served with a thick, sweet peanut sauce. Small rice cakes and cucumber usually accompany the satay. It is served in some restaurants, and at many hawker centers. You can buy ready-made satay sauce to try at home with a barbecue.

CRYSTAL JADE ($$)

crystaljade.com

This Asia-wide chain serves traditional Cantonese cuisine, including fresh seafood, barbecued pork and soups—and arguably the best dim sum in town.

C4 ✉ 04-20 Ngee Ann City, 391 Orchard Road ☎ 6238 1661 ⏰ Daily 11.30–2.30, 6.30–10.30 Ⓜ Orchard

CURE ($$$)

curesingapore.com

Under the direction of chef Andrew Walsh, who cut his teeth at London Michelin-starred restaurants, Cure offers inventive, meticulously plated contemporary cuisine in a stylish, relaxed setting. The menu changes seasonally.

E7 ✉ 21 Keong Saik Road ☎ 6221 2189 ⏰ Mon–Tue, Sat 6–10, Wed–Fri 12–2, 6–10 Ⓜ Outram Park 🚌 61, 166, 197

ESQUINA ($$$)

esquina.com.sg

An anchor tenant of the Keong Saik food scene, this corner, two-story shophouse is one of Singapore's best for contemporary Spanish tapas. The set lunch menus offer great value.

E6 ✉ 16 Jiak Chuan Road ☎ 6222 1616 ⏰ Mon 6–10.30, Tue–Sat 12–2.30, 6–10.30 Ⓜ Chinatown

INDOCHINE ($$$)

indochine-group.com

The original haunt of what is now a global brand is tucked away in Chinatown. Vietnamese, Cambodian and Laotian dishes include spicy sausage and fried fish. There are four other branches in Singapore, including the lavish Forbidden City at Clarke Quay.

E7 ✉ 47 Club Street ☎ 6323 0503 ⏰ Mon–Fri noon–10.30, Sat 6–10.30pm Ⓜ Chinatown

KILO ($$)

kilokitchen.com

Come for dinner and stay for drinks at this industrial-styled Kallang hangout. The well-conceived menu includes everything from raw Japanese-style seafood like wasabi tuna tartare to crispy baby squid and seared scallops.

G4 ✉ 66 Kampong Bugis ☎ 6467 3987 ⏰ Mon–Sat 6pm–midnight Ⓜ Lavender 🚌 2, 7, 12, 13, 32

KOMALA VILAS ($)

komalavilas.com.sg

Vegetarian Indian fare is served here on banana leaves. It's good and inexpensive, and you can have unlimited helpings. Try the sweet, spicy *masala* tea.

F4 ✉ 76–78 Serangoon Road ☎ 6293 6980 ⏰ Daily 7am–10.30pm Ⓜ Little India

LAU PA SAT ($)

laupasat.biz

This 24-hour hawker center's appeal is as much about architecture as it is about good food. There are more than 100 stalls here, housed within the largest remaining Victorian cast-iron building in Asia. Come in the evening, when it's liveliest, for a cold beer and hot satay.

F7 ✉ 18 Raffles Quay ⏰ 24 hours Ⓜ Raffles Place

LOLLA ($$$)

lolla.com.sg

The now-permanent home of what began as an underground pop-up restaurant, Lolla specializes in Mediterranean-inspired tapas often given an Asian twist, like Spanish tortilla with smoked eel or sea urchin pudding. The wine menu is exceptional, too. Grab a counter seat at the first floor's open kitchen to watch the chefs.

🚆 E7 ✉ 22 Ann Siang Road ☎ 6423 1228 🕐 Daily noon–2.30, 6–11 🚇 Chinatown

NATIONAL KITCHEN BY VIOLET OON ($$$)

violetoon.com

Celebrity Singaporean chef Violet Oon presents her signature Peranakan dishes like beef rendang, dry laksa and *ikan goreng* chili at this gorgeous jewel box restaurant in the National Gallery. Her Satay Bar & Grill at Clarke Quay is fantastic, too.

🚆 F6 ✉ 1 St. Andrew's Road, National Gallery, #02-01 ☎ 9834 9935 🕐 Daily noon–2.30, 3–5, 6–10.30 🚇 Esplanade 🚌 195, 961, 961C

PASTA BRAVA ($$)

pastabrava.com.sg

Pasta Brava is a lovely Italian restaurant in a converted shophouse on the edge of Chinatown. Some dishes can be expensive, but the food is very good and is popular with local workers.

🚆 E8 ✉ 11 Craig Road ☎ 6227 7550 🕐 Mon–Sat 11.30–2.30, 6.30–10.30 🚇 Tanjong Pagar

PREGO ($$$)

swissotel.com/hotels/singapore-stamford

This long-established Italian restaurant bustles at lunch and in the evenings thanks to its range of authentic classic dishes and a central location.

🚆 F6 ✉ Swissotel The Stamford, 2 Stamford Road ☎ 6431 5156 🕐 Daily 11.30–2.30, 6.30–10.30 🚇 City Hall

RANG MAHAL ($$$)

rangmahal.com.sg

Serving an excellent range of beautifully presented North Indian dishes, this upscale restaurant swarms during its daily (except Sat) lunch buffet.

🚆 G6 ✉ Level 3, Pan Pacific Hotel, Raffles Boulevard ☎ 6333 1788 🕐 Sun–Fri 12–2.30, 6.30–10.30. Sat 6.30–10.30 🚇 City Hall

RESTAURANT ANDRÉ ($$$)

restaurantandre.com

If you're looking to celebrate a special occasion in style, book a table at André Chiang's stylish eatery, consistently rated one of Asia's top restaurants, to indulge in the nouvelle French set menus.

🚆 D7 ✉ 41 Bukit Pasoh Road ☎ 6534 8880 🕐 Tue–Sat 7–10 🚇 Outram Park 🚌 61, 166, 197

SUPERNATURE ($)

supernature.com.sg

Soy burgers, healthy sandwiches and fresh juices are the staples at this chic organic shop. Vegans will find plenty of appropriate options here.

🚆 C5 ✉ B1-05 Forum, 583 Orchard Road ☎ 6735 4338 🕐 Mon–Sat 10–7, Sun 11–6 🚇 Orchard

YUM CHA ($$)

yumcha.com.sg

Visit on the weekends and select delicious dim sum from push carts. Framed photos of Chinatown in the 1960s give you an idea of what the area was like back in the day.

🚆 E7 ✉ 20 Trengganu Street (off Temple Street), 02-01 ☎ 6372 1717 🕐 Mon–Fri 11–11, Sat–Sun 9am–11pm 🚇 Chinatown

---

POPIAH

Popiah—freshly prepared rice-flour pancakes filled with a mouthwatering mixture of onion, turnip, bean sprouts, minced pork and prawns, all held together with a sweet soy sauce and flavored with cilantro, garlic and chili—make a delicious snack. Many hawker centers have a *popiah* stall.

West Island

Head west for the world's best bird park, a patch of original tropical rainforest, and hedonistic Sentosa, the recreational hub of this dynamic island nation.

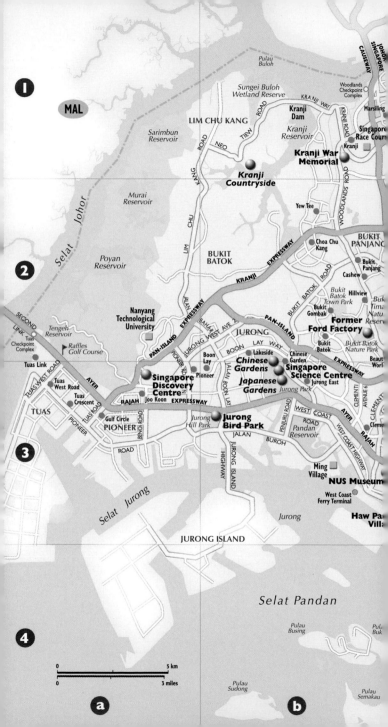

Selat Johor

SEMBAWANG

Sembawan Beach

MAL

ADMIRALTY ROAD

CANBERRA LINK

WOODLANDS AVENUE 7

Sembawang

Admiralty

WOODLANDS AVENUE

Woodlands

WOODLANDS

Pulau Seletar

YISHUN

Yishun

ROAD

Pulau Punggol Barat

Yishun Park

Pulau Punggol Timor

Khatib

SELETAR EXPRESSWAY

MANDAI ROAD

MANDAI AVE

SEMBAWANG ROAD

Lower Seletar Reservoir

Singapore Zoo and River Safari

Night Safari

Upper Seletar Reservoir

UPPER THOMPSON ROAD

Central Catchment Nature Reserve

BUKIT TIMAH EXPRESSWAY

Singapore Nature Reserves

Upper Peirce Reservoir

MacRitchie Trail

PAN-ISLAND

MacRitchie Reservoir

LORNIE ROAD

EXPRESSWAY

TOA PAYOH

King Albert Park

DUNEARN

BUKIT TIMAH

BUKIT TIMAH ROAD

Sixth Avenue

ROAD

Botanic Gardens

ANDAN RD

Tan Kah Kee

Stevens

Dover

HOLLAND ROAD

Farrer Road

Singapore Botanic Gardens

COMMON WEALTH

Holland Village

NAPIER RD

ORCHARD ROAD

Buona Vista

Commonwealth

AVENUE

DEMPSEY HILL

EXPRESSWAY

One North

Kent Ridge

Queenstown

ALEXANDRA ROAD

JALAN BUKIT MERAH

Redhill

Tiong Bahru

WEST

Southern Ridges

Giliman Barracks

Telok Blangah Hill Park

TIONG BAHRU

aw Par illa

Pasir Panjang

COAST HIGHWAY

115

Mount Faber

Labrador Park

Telok Blangah

HarbourFront

GATEWAY AVENUE

Pulau Brani

Universal Studios

Sentosa

Pulau Tekukor

Pulau Seringat

Pulau Tembakul (Kusu Island)

Pulau Jong

Pulau Sakijang Bendera (St John's Island)

Pulau Lazarus (Sakijang Pelepah)

Pulau Sebarok

Pulau Darat

Pulau Subar Laut

c

d

Gillman Barracks

HIGHLIGHTS

- ShanghART Gallery
- The Naked Finn
- Playeum
- Guided tours
- Art After Dark
- Timbre @ Gillman

TIP

- If original artwork is out of your budget, pop into gallery shop Supermama to browse a beautiful collection of gifts and handicrafts crafted by Singaporean and Japanese makers.

These redeveloped military barracks just outside central Singapore are another exciting addition to the city's contemporary arts scene. This is the place to enjoy a day of gallery hopping.

Gallery gazing Sprawling across nearly 16 acres (6.5ha) of green space along the lush Southern Ridges (▷ 75–76) corridor, Gillman Barracks opened in 2012 and instantly became one of Singapore's premier art spaces. Galleries here include the only overseas branch of influential Chinese arts organization ShanghART Gallery. Guided weekly and monthly tours are a great way to hit the highlights. Check the Gillman calendar for special events like the food/music/after-hours party extravaganza Art After Dark, held bi-monthly on a Friday night.

Clockwise from left: there are 13 contemporary art galleries housed in the refurbished colonial barracks; children can get creative in the Playeum Centre; stroll round the site to take in the 16 outdoor murals, sculptures and installations, including Land of Shadows *(2016) by Cleon Peterson*

The biggest party of all is during Singapore Art Week in January.

Art for all ages Not just for discerning arts enthusiasts, however, Gillman also caters to budding artists. Kids aged 12 and under can visit Playeum's Children's Centre for Creativity to engage their senses through a series of interactive exhibitions, educational workshops, art jams and more.

Food for thought Food is never far away in Singapore. Here there are six bars and restaurants, including Timbre @ Gillman, which hosts nightly live music, and The Naked Finn (▷ 80), a contemporary restaurant serving sustainably sourced seafood. Satisfy your sweet tooth at Creamier Handcrafted Ice Cream and Coffee.

THE BASICS

gillmanbarracks.com
🏏 C3
✉ 9 Lock Road
🕐 Varies by gallery; closed Mon
🍴 Bars, restaurants
🚇 Labrador Park
🚌 51, 57, 61, 83, 97
♿ Good
✋ Free. Playeum moderate

HIGHLIGHTS

- Penguin feeding time
- Jungle Jewels
- Pelican Cove
- Waterfall Aviary
- World of Darkness
- Crowned pigeons
- Birds of paradise
- Southeast Asian hornbills and South American toucans

TIP

- The Breeding and Research Centre offers a behind-the-scenes look at how abandoned eggs and chicks are cared for.

Lunching with parrots, mingling with flamingos and watching exotic tropical birds fly at the Waterfall Aviary are just three of the many lures at Singapore's exceptional bird sanctuary.

The world's birds Jurong Bird Park is Asia-Pacific's biggest bird park—49 acres (20ha)—and home to more than 5,000 birds, many from the tropics. Some 380 species, from all over the world, are housed in aviaries and other apparently open enclosures. Hop on board guided trams for a good overview of the park, or wander on foot to see birds close up.

Birds of a feather Not far from the entrance, penguins live in a simulated Antarctic habitat with a swimming area. The vast glass-sided tank

Clockwise from left: African penguins; the Birds 'n' Buddies show; feeding time in the Lory Loft; the park's four walk-in aviaries are its biggest attractions; Flamingo Lake

has windows 98ft (30m) long. The Waterfall Aviary is the most spectacular area, with 5 acres (2ha) of forest contained beneath high netting, with more than 1,500 African birds. The aviary also has a 100ft (30m) man-made waterfall. The Southeast Asian Birds Aviary is good for spotting local species; it re-creates a rainforest, even laying on a simulated storm at midday, and contains more than 260 species, including the colorful parrots. The African Wetlands exhibit, complete with native-style pavilions, includes the shoebill and African crowned crane. Jungle Jewels is a large walk-through aviary devoted to hummingbirds and other South American species. Twice a day, the Birds 'n' Buddies show features comedy, audience interaction and entertaining antics from the park's birds.

THE BASICS

birdpark.com.sg

✚ b3

✉ 2 Jurong Hill

☎ 6265 0022

🕐 Daily 8.30–6

🍴 Bongo Burgers, Hawk Café, Ben & Jerry's

🚇 MRT to Boon Lay then SBS bus 194 or 251

♿ Good

✋ Moderate

❓ Bird shows: Kings of the Skies (10, 4), Birds 'n' Buddies (11, 3), Lunch with Parrots (1)

Night Safari

HIGHLIGHTS

- "Open" enclosures
- Leopard Trail
- Mouse deer
- Tapirs
- Giraffes
- Lions
- Tigers
- Hippos
- Elephants
- Bats
- Walking trails

TIP

- Check the weather forecast before venturing here, since rain spoils the whole experience somewhat.

Singapore's Night Safari, a zoo that allows you to see nocturnal animals close up, is the largest attraction of its kind in the world and uses special lights to simulate moonlight.

A world of animals The night safari is divided into eight geographical zones that are home to the park's 135 species—more than 2,000 animals in all. You can expect to see animals from the Southeast Asian rainforests, the African savanna, the Nepalese river valley, the South American pampas and the jungles of Myanmar (Burma). As in the Singapore Zoo (▷ 70–71), the enclosures are "open" and animals are confined by hidden walls and ditches. Five of these zones have dedicated walking tracks; the others must be visited by tram.

Clockwise from left: close up with the tapirs; the tram is the best way to see the animals; a baby anteater; Chawang, the Asian elephant

Welcome to the jungle The best way to see the Night Safari is to take the tram journey—the tram is silent to avoid frightening the animals. A guide offers commentary as you pass through. Get off at the tram stations and follow the marked walking trails through each zone. You can rejoin the tram anytime; all follow the same route. Avoid using a flash on your camera as it disturbs the animals and fellow visitors.

What to see Listen for the intermittent roaring of the big cats. The Leopard Trail is one of the busiest walking trails. You can see straight into the enclosure of the prowling leopards—only a plate-glass wall separates you from them. The Wallaby Trail is inspired by the Australian Outback, and includes a cave filled with scorpions and venomous centipedes.

THE BASICS

nightsafari.com.sg

✚ c2

✉ 80 Mandai Lake Road

☎ 6269 3411

🕐 Daily 7.30pm–midnight

🍴 Ulu Ulu Restaurant and gourmet Safari Express

Ⓢ Ang Mo Kio, then bus 138 or Choa Chu Kang, then bus 927

♿ Reasonable

💰 Expensive

Sentosa

HIGHLIGHTS

- S.E.A. Aquarium
- Universal Studios
- Cable car
- Resorts World
- Tanjong Beach Club
- Sentosa Cove

TIP

- Visit midweek to avoid the worst of the crowds.

Home to world-class restaurants from celebrity chefs, an amusement park, casino, sprawling spas and even a few swimming beaches, manmade Sentosa island is undoubtedly a place to play.

Fun park Sentosa self-consciously caters to a variety of tastes, so if you're seeking the real Singapore, the island is probably not for you. Land reclamation and massive construction have turned this one-time pirates' lair into the closest thing Singapore has to Disneyland. It's still got a lovely green canopy covering, and there are quiet pockets, but Sentosa has become mass-market. Arrive in style by taking the cable car from Mount Faber or HarbourFront, flying over jungle, beaches and Sentosa's manifold attractions.

Clockwise from left: aerial view of the Resorts World complex; S.E.A. (Southeast Asia) Aquarium; the Mount Faber cable car carries visitors across to the island from Mount Faber peak

Rides and thrills In the past few years the island has filled with even more entertainment. The giant hotel and entertainment hub of Resorts World is home to the S.E.A. Aquarium, Adventure Cove Waterpark, Universal Studios theme park (▷ 76), with its cutting-edge roller coasters, a casino and six hotels. Over on Siloso Beach, adventure-seekers can try out iFly, an indoor skydiving wind tunnel, or the nearby Wave House for a simulated surf experience.

Nightlife Along with all the restaurants that have popped up over the years, nightlife has developed on the island as well. Both Tanjong and Mambo beach clubs offer pool-side bars by the sea, with a variety of DJs visiting the decks regularly. Over at Sentosa Cove, W Hotel is known to throw a good party.

THE BASICS

sentosa.com.sg

✚ c4, arrowed off at B9

✉ Just south of Singapore Island

☎ Sentosa Information Centre 1800 736 8672

🕐 24 hours

🍴 Cafés and restaurants

🚠 Cable car from HarbourFront and Mount Faber (expensive)

🚇 HarbourFront, then take Sentosa Express

♿ Generally good

💷 Individual venues may charge a cover

Singapore Botanic Gardens

HIGHLIGHTS

● Rubber trees
● National Orchid Garden
● Jungle Walk
● Palm Valley
● *Myristica fragans* (nutmeg tree)
● *Cinnamomum zeylanicum* (cinnamon tree)
● Topiary
● Bamboos
● Herbarium

TIP

● Go to sbg.org.sg for details of the free concerts that are held on the Show Foundation Symphony Stage.

Don't leave Singapore without a visit to this botanical wonder, with its splendid National Orchid Garden.

Botanical beginnings Singapore's tranquil botanic gardens are only a few miles from frenetic Orchard Road. Sir Stamford Raffles established botanical gardens at the base of Government Hill in 1822, and the collection was moved to its present site in 1859. Over the decades, the gardens have been enlarged and landscaped. The region's first rubber trees, native to Brazil, were propagated here in 1877, and their descendants remain in the gardens. In the 1960s, the gardens supplied many of the seedlings for roadsides and parks all over the island. Today, the gardens are an important center for plant research and conservation.

Highlights Stroll through the National Orchid Garden (▷ 78) to see the largest display of tropical orchids in the world—more than 1,000 species and 2,000 hybrids—with a Cool House for high-altitude orchids and displays with orchids in natural settings. The Ginger Garden has over 500 species, including plants that you probably never thought were related to ginger, such as bananas. On the rolling lawn of Palm Valley you'll find groups of palms, while the nearby patch of tropical rainforest is one of the few remaining areas of Singapore's original vegetation. Australian black swans and other water birds live around the Eco-Lake, where there are displays of herbs and spices, medicinal plants, fruit trees and bamboos. The gardens are popular with locals, who come here to jog, picnic and attend the open-air concerts.

THE BASICS

sbg.org.sg
✚ c3, A4
✉ 1 Cluny Road
☎ 6471 7361
🕐 Daily 5am–midnight; National Orchid Garden daily 8.30am–7pm
🍴 Cafés and restaurants
🚇 Botanic Gardens
🚌 7, 75, 105, 106, 123, 174
♿ Good
💵 Botanic Gardens free; Orchid Garden inexpensive

Singapore Nature Reserves

TOP
25

Singapore is renowned for its green open spaces and, given its size, there are a surprising number of reserves where the original vegetation remains.

Bukit Timah The last remaining area of primary tropical rainforest in Singapore covers 410 acres (166ha) of Bukit Timah, Singapore's highest hill at 538ft (164m). Color-coded trails that start at the visitor area allow you to observe the reserve's fauna and flora, and a mountain bike trail is available for the more adventurous traveler.

MacRitchie Reservoir Park You can jog or walk on the shaded paths around the reservoir's edge; there are exercise stations at intervals. The highlight of several walks through the park,

Clockwise from left: Bukit Timah; MacRitchie Reservoir Park; boardwalk at Sungei Buloh nature reserve

the TreeTop Walk is along a freestanding suspension bridge that connects the park's two highest points. If it's not too busy, you can spot several animals along the way, including monitor lizards and fish eagles as well as long-tailed macaques, so don't have any food in sight.

Sungei Buloh Singapore's only wetland nature reserve covers 312 acres (130ha). Carefully planned walkways and strategically placed hides allow you to explore swamp, mangrove and mudflat habitats, and to observe tropical birdlife and marine creatures, particularly mudskippers and crabs. Early morning and evening are the best times for viewing wildlife, with bird life most evident before 10am. From September to March, migratory birds from as far afield as eastern Siberia stop over here.

THE BASICS

nparks.gov.sg
Bukit Timah
✚ b2
✉ 177 Hindhede Drive
☎ 6468 5736
🕐 Daily 6am–7pm
🚇 MRT to Newton, then SBS bus 171 or TIBS 182, 65, 67, 75, 170, 171, 852, 961
♿ None
💷 Free

MacRitchie Reservoir Park
✚ c2
✉ Lornie Road
🕐 24 hours
🍴 Food kiosk
🚇 MRT to Newton, then bus 104, 132 or 167
♿ Good
💷 Free

Sungei Buloh
sbwr.org.sg
✚ b1
✉ 301 Neo Tiew Crescent
☎ 6794 1401
🕐 Mon–Sat 7.30–7, Sun 7–7
🚌 Take SMRT Bus 925 from Kranji MRT Station. Alight at Kranji Reservoir car park and walk for 15 min
♿ Good
💷 Mon–Fri free; Sat, Sun inexpensive

Singapore Zoo and River Safari

HIGHLIGHTS

- "Open" enclosures
- Tigers, including the Bengal White
- Pygmy hippos
- Primate islands
- Treetops Trail
- Komodo dragons
- Children's World
- Tram
- River Safari

TIP

- Consider a Park Hopper 3-in-1 ticket for the zoo, Night Safari and Jurong Bird Park.

Start your day with a buffet breakfast in the jungle with orangutans, then explore one of Asia's greatest zoos before embarking on an unforgettable river cruise with manatees.

The zoo Singapore's zoo, acclaimed as one of the finest in the world, is also one of the youngest. Its beginnings can be traced back to the 1960s, when British forces pulled out of Singapore and left a ragbag of family pets behind. The zoo, which sprawls over 69 acres (28ha), was officially opened in 1973 and is now home to more than 300 species, some endangered and rare, such as tigers, orangutans, Komodo dragons and golden lion tamarins, kept in as natural conditions as possible. Breeding programs have been initiated for

Clockwise from far left: elephant feeding time; river safari viewing deck; the leopard enclosure is one of the highlights; keep an eye out for the zebras

endangered species, with some success. A tram (extra charge) trundles round the grounds to save you some walking.

River Safari This S$160-million attraction is Asia's first river-themed safari park. The ambitious concept is divided into different zones dedicated to the Mississippi, Congo, Nile, Ganges, Murray, Mekong and Yangtze rivers—guests stroll through the park and encounter wildlife native to these bodies of water. The park hosts Southeast Asia's largest panda exhibit, home of Kai Kai and Jia Jia, and the world's largest freshwater aquarium. Be sure to take a ride on the Amazon River Quest, a boat adventure that floats past more than 30 species of animal, including giant anteaters and jaguars. Be prepared: you will get wet!

THE BASICS

zoo.com.sg
riversafari.com.sg
✚ C2, arrowed off at D1
✉ 80 Mandai Lake Road
☎ 6269 3411
🕐 Zoo daily 8.30–6. River Safari daily 9–6
🍴 Restaurants
🚇 Ang Mo Kio, then SBS bus 138, or Choa Chu Kang then TIBS 927
🚌 SBS bus 171 to Mandai Road then cross road and take 138 or 927
♿ Good
💰 Expensive

More to See

CHINESE AND JAPANESE GARDENS

jtc.gov.sg

Chinese and Japanese classical gardens have been created on two islands in Jurong Lake. The Chinese Garden covers 32 acres (13ha) and is dotted with pagodas, pavilions and arched bridges. The main building is based on Beijing's Summer Palace. During the mid-autumn festival the gardens are hung with lanterns. The Bridge of Double Beauty leads to the Japanese Gardens, which are altogether more serene, and take their inspiration from gardens of the 15th to 17th centuries with their Zen rock gardens, shrubs, lanterns and ponds.

🔲 b3 ✉ 1 Chinese Garden Road ☎ 6261 3632 🕐 Daily 6am–11pm 🍴 Refreshment kiosks 🚇 Chinese Garden 💲 Inexpensive

FORMER FORD FACTORY

nas.gov.sg/formerfordfactory

This art deco-style building, originally Ford's first assembly plant in Asia, is now refurbished as a gallery showing the exhibition "Syonan Years: Singapore Under Japanese Rule, 1942–1945."

The compelling exhibition, curated by the National Archives of Singapore, provides the background of World War II in Malaya and describes the hardships people endured during the Japanese Occupation from 1942 to 1945. The pathway leading to the building was the ceremonial route taken by the British forces on the day of the surrender to the Japanese, and you enter the exhibition gallery through a tunnel, starting at the historic Board Room, where the signing of the surrender took place. The factory was then handed over to Nissan to manufacture military vehicles for the Japanese war effort. On display are archival photographs, oral history interviews, maps and artifacts from the era. On the mezzanine floor is a cinema showing documentaries on various aspects of the period.

Bonsai Garden at the Chinese Gardens

Ten Courts of Hell, Haw Par Villa

🔲 b2 ✉ 351 Upper Bukit Timah Road
☎ 6462 6724 🕐 Mon–Sat 9–5.30,
Sun noon–5.30 🚇 Clementi, then SBS
184 🚌 SBS Bus 170 ♿ Reasonable
🍴 Inexpensive

HAW PAR VILLA
(TIGER BALM GARDENS)

hawparvilla.sg

Brothers Aw Boon Haw and Aw
Boon Par built themselves a villa
here in 1937 after making their
fortune with Tiger Balm curative
ointment. The house is no longer
there, but the gardens are filled
with over 1,000 rather gaudy statues and tableaux based on Chinese
legends and real crimes in old
Singapore. The Ten Courts of Hell
exhibit depicts gory graphic scenes
of punishment handed out to evil-
doers, such as disembowelment or
being plunged into a giant wok of
boiling oil. Strange, yes, but undeni-
ably fascinating.

🔲 c3 ✉ 262 Pasir Panjang Road ☎ 6872
2780 🕐 Daily 9–7 🍴 Cafés 🚇 Buona
Vista, then bus 200 🍴 Free

KRANJI COUNTRYSIDE

kranjicountryside.com

The Kranji Countryside Association
was formed in 2005 to promote
the rural northwest of the island,
opening farms up to the public so
locals and visitors can find out more
about where their food actually
comes from. The association
operates the Kranji Countryside
Express Bus, which brings travelers
from the Kranji MRT station to
nearby farms and Sungei Buloh
Nature Reserve. You can hop on
and off the bus as many times as
you like. There's also a Heritage
Trail around the area, which takes in
a number of historical sites. Come
for a leisurely lunch at Bollywood
Veggies, then spend the afternoon
wandering through the 10 acres
(4ha) of grounds, which also
include a Food Museum.

🔲 b1 ✉ Bollywood Veggies, 100 Neo
Tiew Road ☎ 6261 3632 🕐 Wed–Sun
9–6 🍴 Several farms have restaurants
🚇 Kranji, then Kranji Countryside Express
Bus 🍴 Inexpensive

Former Ford Factory

KRANJI WAR MEMORIAL

The War Memorial is dedicated to the service personnel from Malaya, India, Sri Lanka, Australia, New Zealand, Britain and Canada who died defending Singapore and Malaya against the Japanese during World War II. Two of Singapore's past presidents also lie here. More than 4,000 graves stand in rows along the well-kept lawns, and the names of those whose bodies were not recovered (more than 24,000) are inscribed on the sides of the memorial's 12 walls. The cemetery, a hospital burial ground during the occupation, became a military cemetery after the war.

➕ b1 ✉ 9 Woodlands Road 🕐 Daily 7am–6pm 🚇 Kranji 🚌 SBS bus 170 from Rochor Road ✋ Free

NUS MUSEUM

nus.edu.sg/museum

The center manages Singapore National University's three art collections. The Chinese art collection, located at lobby level in the Lee Kong Chian Art Museum, has six galleries of paintings, calligraphy, ceramics and bronze objects representing every major era of China's long and illustrious history.

The South and Southeast Asian collection, at concourse level in the South and Southeast Asian Gallery, displays artworks that span classical to modern traditions in drawing and painting, textiles, ceramics, sculptures and bronzes from around the region. Some of the works display historic traditions but there's plenty to keep fans of modern Asian art happy, including contemporary paintings, and textiles acquired during recent field trips.

The Ng Eng Teng collection, at the top level in the Ng Eng Teng Gallery, contains more than 1,000 items—figurative sculptures, vessels, ceramic forms, paintings and drawings—by the eponymous Ng, Singapore's foremost sculptor (1934–2001).

➕ b3 ✉ University Cultural Centre Annex, 50 Kent Ridge Crescent, National University

Visionarium, Singapore Discovery Centre

of Singapore ☎ 6516 8817 🕐 Tue–Sat 10–7.30, Sun 10–6 🚇 Clementi, then bus 96 💵 Free

SINGAPORE DISCOVERY CENTRE

sdc.com.sg

The innovative high-tech exhibits at this excellent "edutainment" attraction present macro views of Singapore's past, present and future through a series of brilliant light and sound shows and hands-on activities. One highlight is the world's first and largest interactive team-based city design studio, the Visionarium, where up to 120 visitors at a time can design a new model of Singapore and see it displayed on a huge 360-degree screen. There's also a multi-tiered paintball arena, digital dance studio, crisis simulation theater, 4D simulator ride and 344-seat movie theater with a five-story-high screen.

🔼 a3 ✉ 510 Upper Jurong Road ☎ 6792 6188 🕐 Tue–Sun 9–6 🍴 Cafeteria 🚇 Joo Koon 🦽 Good 💵 Moderate

SIngapore Science Centre

SINGAPORE SCIENCE CENTRE

science.edu.sg

The world of science awaits at the Singapore Science Centre, where more than 1,000 exhibits and hundreds of hands-on displays attract upward of a million annual visitors. Theme galleries offer fascinating insight into human achievements in the physical and life sciences, while nature-focused exhibits like Climate Change Climate Challenge explore global warming and other environmental issues. Other highlights here include laser and mirror mazes, Phobia[2]—The Science of Fear, an interactive flight simulator and regular stargazing sessions at the planetarium. This is a perfect place for a fun-filled family outing.

🔼 b3 ✉ 15 Science Centre Road ☎ 6425 2500 🕐 Daily 10–6 🍴 Cafés and restaurants 🚇 Jurong East then 500yd/m walk (turn left from station, along Block 135) or bus 335 🚌 66, 178, 198 direct; 51, 78, 197 to Jurong East Interchange then bus 335 or walk 🦽 Good 💵 Moderate

SOUTHERN RIDGES

nparks.gov.sg

For a relaxing change of pace, head to the scenic Southern Ridges, which encompass more than 6 miles (10km) of trails and bridges winding through lush tropical greenery near Singapore's southwestern coast. Start at Mount Faber Park, where you can take a roundtrip cable car ride to Sentosa, and head west to at least Kent Ridge Park. Along the way you'll walk the wave-shaped Henderson Waves pedestrian bridge, zig-zag through secondary rainforest on an

elevated metal walkway and stroll through lovely HortPark, which has a number of gardening exhibits and restaurant.

➕ c3 ✉ Mount Faber Road ☎ 6377 9688 🍴 Restaurants, vending machines ♿ No wheelchair access 💷 Park free; cable car moderate

TIONG BAHRU

Within easy walking distance of Chinatown, this laid-back community is Singapore's oldest public housing estate. It's a joy to wander Tiong Bahru's quiet residential streets, which are filled with retro art deco-style architecture unique to the island; indeed, many of these buildings are now protected by the Singapore Urban Redevelopment Authority. Thanks to an influx in recent years of fashionable cafés, indie boutiques and late-night hangouts, Tiong Bahru has become one of the Lion City's most happening 'hoods, and the market is a great place to grab a casual lunch.

➕ C7 ✉ Tiong Bahru Road 🍴 Cafés, bars, restaurants 🚊 Tiong Bahru 🚌 5, 16, 33, 63, 121 💷 Free

UNIVERSAL STUDIOS

rwsentosa.com

Located on Sentosa, this is the only Universal Studios theme park in Southeast Asia. Standout rides include sci-fi-themed Battlestar Galactica: HUMAN vs. CYLON, which features the world's tallest dueling roller coasters, and the Revenge of the Mummy, where riders are besieged by an army of warrior mummies in pitch darkness. The Jurassic Park Rapids Adventure, an outdoor river-raft ride filled with modern animatronic dinosaurs, features a thrilling white-water drop. Special events are held throughout the year, including to celebrate the Lunar New Year and Halloween.

➕ c4 ✉ 8 Sentosa Gateway ☎ 6577 8888 🕐 Daily 10–7; extended hours some weekends 🍴 Abundant options 🚊 HarbourFront, then Sentosa Express ♿ Good 💷 Expensive

Entrance to Revenge of the Mummy ride, Universal Studios

A walk through the Botanic Gardens

This walk takes you through the National Orchid Garden (▷ 66–67); a good time to start is around opening hour (8.30am).

DISTANCE: 1–1.5 miles (1.5–2.5km) **ALLOW:** 2–3 hours

START ⋯⋯⋯

END

TANGLIN GATE (MAIN GATE)

➕ A3, A4, 🚇 Botanic Gardens 🚌 7, 75, 105, 106, 123, 174

TANGLIN GATE OR VISITOR CENTRE

1 Take the path to the left that leads to the March Garden ponds. These lovely ponds, created out of a natural wetland, feature local and non-native water plants.

2 Keep walking to the left around the ponds and follow some stepping stones. Take the turn to the right and walk along to Swan Lake, with its resident white swans and exuberant "Swing Me Mama" sculpture.

3 Continue walking straight ahead until several paths meet and you can see three sets of steps. Take the middle steps to the Sundial Garden—you'll see a Floral Clock on the far side.

4 Climb the steps to the left of the Floral Clock and turn left. Keep going and you'll reach the Sun Rockery, and a little farther on there is a display of the gorgeous *Vanda* Miss Joaquim orchid, the national flower of Singapore.

8 Walk downhill to leave the Orchid Garden. Stroll down the lawn at Palm Valley and admire the palms, then relax by Symphony Lake, before walking up to the Visitor Centre.

7 Down the hill to the right you'll find a huge collection of bromeliads, and the Cool House nearby that houses tropical montane orchid species. From here you loop back up to the Orchidarium, with its lowland species.

6 A path from the Ginger Garden will take you directly to the Orchid Plaza and National Orchid Garden. Turn right once you're inside the gardens and walk to the fountain. Turn left here and walk uphill to the Tan Hoon Siang Misthouse.

5 When you reach the end of the orchid display, you'll see an extremely tall forest tree—walk down the path at its side and along to the Ginger Garden, home to plants in the ginger family and related species.

Shopping

ANTIQUES OF THE ORIENT

aoto.com.sg

You could spend hours browsing through this shop's fine selection of old lithographs, prints, maps and books.

🔢 B4 ✉ 02-40 Tanglin Shopping Centre, 19 Tanglin Road ☎ 6734 9351 🕐 Mon–Sat 10–6, Sun 11–4 🚇 Orchard

BOOKSACTUALLY

booksactuallyshop.com

This indie bookshop is a pleasure to browse. Look for a fantastic selection of rare books and works by local authors, and don't miss the vintage bric-a-brac section in the back.

🔢 C7 ✉ 9 Yong Siak Street ☎ 6222 9195 🕐 Sun–Mon 10–6, Tue–Sat 10–8 🚇 Tiong Bahru

RESORTS WORLD SENTOSA LUXURY FASHION GALLERIA

sentosa.com.sg

Forming a linkway between three of Resorts World Sentosa's major hotels, luxury jewelers, watch-making brands and leading fashion houses line this stretch of high-end retail space.

🔢 A9 ✉ 8 Sentosa Gateway ☎ 6723 8000 🕐 Daily 11–10.30 🚇 Harbourfront, then Sentosa Express

STRANGELETS

strangelets.sg

This funky Tiong Bahru design shop stocks fashion, backpacks, jewelry, notebooks and other assorted items.

🔢 C7 ✉ 7 Yong Siak Street ☎ 6222 1456 🕐 Mon–Fri 11–8, Sat–Sun 10–8 🚇 Tiong Bahru

TANGLIN MALL

tanglinmall.com.sg

This shopping mall provides something a little different from the designer labels on offer on Orchard Road. The range of stores includes some interesting children's shops, a sports shop and three floors of Food Junction.

🔢 B4 ✉ 163 Tanglin Road ☎ 6736 4922 🕐 Daily 10–10 🚇 Orchard

TANGLIN SHOPPING CENTRE

tanglinsc.com

One of the area's oldest shopping malls, this is known for Asian antiques and curios (though, as elsewhere in Singapore, prices are high). It is also good for carpets, tailoring, cameras and accessories.

🔢 B4 ✉ 19 Tanglin Road ☎ 6737 0849 🕐 Mon–Sat 12–6 🚇 Orchard

VIVOCITY

vivocity.com.sg

Singapore's biggest mall is a stunning retail and leisure complex on the waterfront, with department stores (including Tangs) and brand-name shops, plus restaurants, cinemas and a hypermarket.

🔢 c4 ✉ 1 HarbourFront Walk ☎ 6377 6860 🕐 Daily 10–10 🚇 HarbourFront

CARPET AUCTIONS

Taking in a carpet auction can be a fun way to spend a Sunday. Several carpet companies hold auctions then, usually at the Hyatt, the Hilton or the Holiday Inn. Carpets are spread out for easy viewing from about 10 until just after noon. Estimated market prices are posted and a Continental-type buffet breakfast is often free to participants. Auctions usually start about 1. Depending on the number of viewers and the size of their wallets, bidding proceeds at a fast pace. Expect to get 50–70 percent off the estimated price, or at least start the bidding there.

Where to Eat

PRICES		
Prices are approximate, based on a 3-course meal for one person.		
$$$	over S$60	
$$	S$30–S$60	
$	under S$30	

2AM:DESSERTBAR

2amdessertbar.com

This chic 60-seat dessert/cocktail bar, discreetly located in expat enclave Holland Village, is where it all started for acclaimed Singaporean pastry chef Janice Wong. Here she pairs imaginative, artfully presented desserts, ranging from tiramisu to green tea tart, with handcrafted cocktails. There's a small range of savory dishes, too.

➕ c3 ✉ 21A Lorong Liput ☎ 6291 9727 🕐 Tue–Fri 3pm–2am, Sat–Sun 2pm–2am 🚇 Holland Village

DEMPSEY HILL ($–$$$)

dempseyhill.com

Tucked away near the Botanic Gardens, these former army barracks are now home to some of the city's top restaurants. Long Beach is famed for its chili and black pepper crabs, while nearby RedDot BrewHouse is one of Singapore's best brewpubs. Blu Kouzina (Mediterranean), The Dempsey Cookhouse and Bar (European) and Candlenut (Peranakan) are all recommended, as well.

➕ Off map A4 ✉ Dempsey Road 🚌 Shuttle bus from Holland Village or Botanic Gardens

THE NAKED FINN ($$$)

nakedfinn.com

Fresh, sustainable seafood like wild baby Indian squid and locally farmed barramundi are prepared and presented with minimal fuss—and that's the beauty of this buzzy Gillman Barracks eatery. Both à la carte and set tasting menus for large groups are available.

➕ c3 ✉ Block 39, Malan Road, Gillman Barracks ☎ 6694 0807 🕐 Tue–Thu 12–3, 6–10, Fri–Sat 12–3, 6–10.30 🚇 Holland Village

O'COFFEE CLUB ($)

ocoffeeclub.com

The O'Coffee Club chain specializes in interesting coffees, some with cream and a choice of spirits, and also serves pastas, salads and sandwiches.

➕ A4 ✉ 48 Lorong Mambong ☎ 6466 0296 🕐 Mon–Sat 11am–midnight, Sun 10am–midnight 🚇 Holland Village

SAMY'S CURRY ($)

samyscurry.com

Located in a former civil-service clubhouse, with a colonial edifice and overhead fans; meals here are served on banana leaves. Try spoonfuls of zesty curries, fragrant rices, breads and assorted condiments.

➕ A4 ✉ 25 Dempsey Road ☎ 6472 2080 🕐 Daily 11–3, 6–10

COFFEE SHOPS
Singapore's traditional coffee shops are nothing like the modern places that sell a sophisticated selection of lattes and pastries. They are no-nonsense, cheap-and-cheerful-options for popular local rice and noodle dishes. You also get coffee, locally referred to as *"kopi,"* but it's thick and sweet, made with condensed milk. Mindful of waste, coffee shops sometimes serve takeout coffee in empty condensed-milk cans, though the more usual coffee container today is the familiar Styrofoam container or a plastic bag, which you can sometimes see tied to railings while the contents cool.

The east of Singapore has long, sandy beaches lined with excellent seafood restaurants, recreational water sports, including a cable ski park, poignant World War II memorials and historic temples.

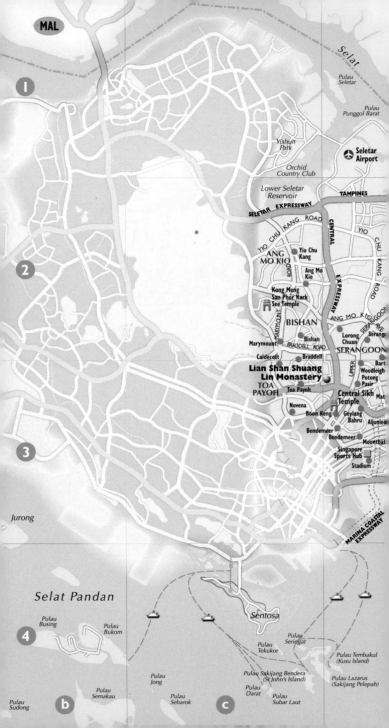

MAL

Johor

Pulau
Punggol Timor

Pulau
Serangoon

Mamam Beach

Pulau
Tekong
Kechil

PUNGGOL

Punggol
EXPRESSWAY

Coney Island
Beach

Chek Jawa
Wetlands

Pulau Ubin

Pulau Ubin
Park

Changi
Beach

engkang

Pulau
Ketam

Pulau Ubin
Ferry Terminal

SENGKANG

Buangkok

HOUGANG

Hougang

TAMPINES

PASIR RIS

Serangoon
Harbour

Pasir Ris
Beach

Pasir Ris
Park

Changi
Village

CHANGI

Changi Ferry
Terminal

KALLANG PAYA
LEBAR EXPRESSWAY

PUNGGOL ROAD

Pasir Ris

EXPRESSWAY

LOYANG AVENUE

Changi
International
Airport

TAMPINES

AIRPORT RD

TAMPINES AVENUE 10

Tampines
East

Tampines

Changi
Airport

The Changi
Museum

EAST COAST PARKWAY

van

BARTLEY RD

Bedok
Reservoir

Tampines
West

TAMPINES

EAST

PAN-

ISLAND EXPRESSWAY

SIMEI

Simei

SIMEI AVE

Upper
Changi

CHANGI ROAD

Kaki
Bukit

Bedok
North

Bedok
Reservoir

Simei

ROAD

Changi
Expo

XILIN AVENUE

CHANGI
EAST

Ubi

MacPherson

Kembangan

NEW UPPER

CHANGI ROAD

Eunos

BEDOK

Bedok

Tanah
Merah

Newater
Visitor
Centre

Tanah Merah
Ferry Terminal

aya
bar
Dakota

GEYLANG

Betel Box
Tours

EAST COAST ROAD

PARKWAY

EAST

National
Sailing Centre

oo Chiat
Road

EAST

COAST

East Coast Beach

Bedok
Jetty

Spark Sea
Adventure Park

Marine Cove

East Coast
Park

0   5 km

0   3 miles

d   e

East Island

East Coast Park

HIGHLIGHTS

- Big Splash
- Kayak rental
- East Coast Sailing Centre
- SKI360°
- Mana Mana
- Xtreme Skate Park

TIP

- Singapore's freshest seafood can be found at the waterfront eateries, but avoid Sunday, when they are always packed.

Two decades of land reclamation have created this beachside playground. Swim or sail; walk, jog or cycle the 6 miles (10km) of tracks between coconut groves; or simply laze on white sands.

Plenty to do Picnicking families flock to the area on the weekends. There are many places to rent a bicycle, kayak or rollerblades, and it's a pleasant place to relax and catch a cooling breeze in the evening. The East Coast Seafood Centre houses several excellent seafood restaurantd and is very popular, although it does lose some of the beach ambience amid a large concrete plaza. The East Coast Lagoon Food Village farther east is another popular spot, and feels slightly more down to earth and natural.

Clockwise from left: cycling along the promenade; the cable ski park; you can also rent bicycles here; beach scene

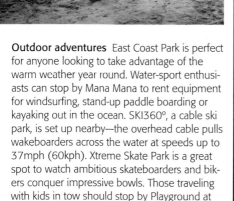

Outdoor adventures East Coast Park is perfect for anyone looking to take advantage of the warm weather year round. Water-sport enthusiasts can stop by Mana Mana to rent equipment for windsurfing, stand-up paddle boarding or kayaking out in the ocean. SKI360°, a cable ski park, is set up nearby—the overhead cable pulls wakeboarders across the water at speeds up to 37mph (60kph). Xtreme Skate Park is a great spot to watch ambitious skateboarders and bikers conquer impressive bowls. Those traveling with kids in tow should stop by Playground at Big Splash, where you'll find an indoor mini golf course modeled after Singapore landmarks.

Beaches The 12 miles (20km) of beaches are popular on weekends, but swimming in the often murky waters is not advised.

THE BASICS

nparks.gov.sg

➕ d3, J5 to M5

✉ East Coast Service Road

☎ ECSC 6449 5118. Big Splash 6345 1321. SKI360° 6442 7318

🍴 East Coast Lagoon Food Village and Jumbo Seafood (▷ 92), various kiosks, fast food at Marina Cove and Big Splash

🚇 Bedok, then bus 31, 197 or 401; Eunos, then 55, 155; Paya Lebar, then 76, 135 and walk

🚌 16, 31, 55, 76, 135, 155, 196, 197, 853 daily to Marine Parade Road; 401 to East Coast Service Road (Sun)

♿ Some level paths

🆓 Free; rental charges per hour for sports, etc

More to See

BETEL BOX TOURS

betelbox.com

As well as serving as a reliable hostel, playing host to many a backpacker over the years, Betel Box also began the Real Singapore Tours. One of the most popular is the Joo Chiat/Katong Food Walk, where visitors are led through some of the best local eateries, being introduced to Singaporean cuisine and taught about local customs. They also offer several bike tours, nature walks and even a pub crawl. All tours begin at the Betel Box hostel on Joo Chiat Road.

🔒 d3 ✉ 200 Joo Chiat Road ☎ 6247 7340 🕐 Days and times vary 🚇 Paya Lebar 💷 Prices vary

CHANGI MUSEUM

changimuseum.sg

Portraying the horrific conditions the more than 50,000 incarcerated civilians, Allied troops and prisoners endured during World War II, the Changi Museum presents a sobering reminder of Singapore's turbulent past. Photographs, letters, drawings and personal effects of many prisoners are displayed, and regular screenings of short films are held. Audio tours are available, and those interested in diving deeper into Singapore's World War II history can join a weekly guided tour with stops at various points of interest across the island; check the museum's website for details.

🔒 e2 ✉ 1000 Upper Changi Road North ☎ 6214 2451 🕐 Daily 9.30–5 🚇 Tanah Merah, then SBS bus 2 ♿ Good 💷 Free

JOO CHIAT ROAD

This once quiet seaside village is today an eclectic mix of colonial villas, Peranakan-style terraces and Malay bungalows, some of which have been renovated while others remain untouched. The Joo Chiat Complex and Geylang Serai market, both at the northern end of Joo Chiat near Malay Village, are good places to find fabrics, household goods and traditional Asian souvenirs at bargain prices. After

Joo Chiat Road

Changi Museum chapel notice board

shopping, refuel at one of the area's many casual Vietnamese restaurants, then cool down with a cold craft beer or cider at the Cider Pit (▷ 91) or Smokey's BBQ (▷ 92). 🚩 d3 ✉ Joo Chiat Road 🍴 Cafés, bars, restaurants 🚇 Paya Lebar then walk 🚌 16, 33 💷 Free

LIAN SHAN SHUANG LIN MONASTERY

shuanglin.sg

Rather incongruously set amid HDB (Housing and Development Board) residential towers, this magnificent temple is a national monument to Singapore's Chinese immigrants, built between 1868 and 1908 and renovated in 2002. The architecture incorporates elements of the building styles of Fujian province, in southeast China, from where the original laborers came. The seven-floor gold-topped pagoda is a replica of the one at the 800-year-old Shanfeng temple in Fujian. The main Mahariva Hall is supported by colorful beams, decorated with carvings. At the back of the complex is the oldest building here—a small wooden shrine containing murals of the much-loved Chinese legend "Journey to the West."
🚩 d3 ✉ 184E Jalan Toa Payoh ☎ 6259 6924 🕐 Daily 6.30am–9pm 🚇 Toa Payoh 💷 Free

PASIR RIS PARK

nparks.gov.sg

This 175-acre (71ha) area lying at the end of the East–West MRT line contains some of Singapore's last remaining stretches of mangrove swamp, and is now a bird and nature reserve. Raised boardwalks meander through this habitat. Look for fiddler crabs, mudskippers and small-clawed otters. Birds you might spot include herons, yellow-vented bulbuls, brown-throated sunbirds and collared kingfishers. You can also walk or cycle direct to East Coast Park from here along the connecting path.
🚩 e2 ✉ Off Jalan Loyang Kecil 🕐 Daily 24 hours 🚇 Pasir Ris, then bus 403 💷 Free

Pasir Ris Park mangrove boardwalk

East Coast Park Walk

This recreational park (▷ 84–85) running for 12 miles (20km) along the East Coast, has water sports and seafood restaurants.

DISTANCE: 1–1.5 miles (1.5–2.5km) **ALLOW:** 2–3 hours

START

BUS STOP

🚏 d3 🚍 Bedok then bus 31, 197 or 401; Eunos then 55, 155, 196 to Marine Crescent and Marine Terrace

1 Walk to the lagoon, where you can watch cable-skiers of all ages practice their wakeboarding skills at SKI360°. Bring your bathing suit and have a go!

2 When you're finished, head north up the beach to the East Coast Lagoon Food Centre, a popular hawker area, for a cool, fresh tropical fruit drink and an exotic snack.

3 Continue on up the beach to the nearby Mana Mana and rent a paddle board or kayak, or just sit in the shade and watch the action.

END

BUS STOP

6 Take a walk farther down the beach or a quiet nap under a beach-side coconut tree before you return to the bus stop for the trip back to the Bedok Interchange or Eunos.

5 By now you should have worked up a real appetite, so head south down the beach to the East Coast Seafood Centre, where there are many restaurants specializing in seafood. Try the local favorites—crispy baby octopus, drunken prawns and chili crab—wonderful!

4 If there's not much wind, you can rent a dinghy a bit farther up the beach and row to the nearby Bedok Jetty, which is popular with recreational fisherfolk.

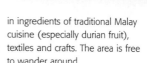

Shopping

112 KATONG

112katong.com.sg

Located at the intersection of East Coast and Joo Chiat roads, this six-level mall has more than 150 shops, as well as a roof garden with a wet playground for the kids.

➕ M4 ✉ 112 East Coast Road ☎ 6636 2112 🕐 Daily 10–10 🚇 Paya Lebar, then free shuttle bus 🚌 10, 10E, 12, 14, 14E, 16, 32, 40

CENTURY SQUARE AND TAMPINES MALL

centurysquare.com.sg

These malls are hugely popular with Tampines residents and convenient for a last-minute splurge before leaving from Changi Airport.

➕ e2 ✉ 2-4 Tampines Central ☎ 6789 6261; 6788 8370 🚇 Tampines

CHANGI CITY POINT

changicitypoint.com.sg

Particularly convenient for those staying near the airport on a quick overnight stay, this massive and modern shopping mall houses factory outlets of familiar international brands, a supermarket and a food court.

➕ e2 ✉ 5 Changi Business Park ☎ 6511 1088 🚇 Expo

CITY PLAZA

cityplaza.sg

This is a great mall for bargain hunters, with many budget and secondhand fashion outlets, and is also home to the legendary Arnold's Fried Chicken.

➕ L3 ✉ 810 Geylang Road ☎ 6748 2320 🕐 Mon–Sat 10.30–8, Sun 9–9 🚇 Paya Lebar

GEYLANG SERAI

Located in Geylang, this is the cultural heart of the Malay community in Singapore. The shops here specialize in ingredients of traditional Malay cuisine (especially durian fruit), textiles and crafts. The area is free to wander around.

➕ d3 ✉ Geylang Serai ☎ 6294 7559 🕐 Daily 10–10 🚇 Paya Lebar

PARKWAY PARADE

parkwayparade.com.sg

This is a handy mall if you're visiting East Coast Park, with a Giant hypermarket and good range of brand-name stores, including Harvey Norman for electronics, Marks & Spencer and Japanese department store Isetan.

➕ M5 ✉ 80 Marine Parade Road ☎ 6344 1242 🕐 Daily 10–10 🚇 Bedok then free shuttle bus (weekends only) 🚌 15, 31, 36, 43, 48, 135, 196, 197

RUMAH BEBE

rumahbebe.com

Discover new bits of Peranakan history in this shophouse, dedicated to the preservation of traditional arts and showcasing this unique culture. Browse the selection of brightly colored clothing, shoes and accessories, or take a tour.

➕ M4 ✉ 113 East Coast Road ☎ 6247 8781 🕐 Tue–Sun 9.30–6.30 🚌 10, 10E, 12, 14, 14E, 16, 32, 40

ANTIQUES

Furniture and objects more than 100 years old, considered antiques, are sold in a plethora of antiques and reproduction shops. Buy only from reputable dealers. They will give a certificate of antiquity or a detailed description, along with a receipt. This proof may be required to ensure duty-free importation to the US and UK. Prices are usually lower in the country of origin than in Singapore; they vary widely here, and bargaining is essential.

Entertainment and Nightlife

CHANGI SAILING CLUB

csc.org.sg

Although a private club and a long way out of town, this makes a lovely, relaxing place for an evening drink and meal on the small balcony overlooking the beach, under the palm trees or in the comfortable bar. Nonmembers are admitted for a dollar Monday to Friday evenings.

➕ e3 ✉ 32 Netheravon Road ☎ 6545 2876 🕐 Restaurant daily 10–10 🚇 Tampines, then bus 29

THE CIDER PIT

In a city with some of the highest beer prices in the region, this no-frills watering hole does a steady trade thanks to its reasonable pricing and stellar selection of imported craft ciders and beers. Traditional British pub food is served, too.

➕ M4 ✉ 328 Joo Chiat Road ☎ 6440 0504 🕐 Mon–Fri 5pm–1am, Sat–Sun 1pm–1am 🚇 Eunos 🚌 16, 33

DOWNTOWN EAST

downtowneast.com.sg

This giant theme park-cum-resort has lots of entertainment choices at affordable prices: food courts, retail shopping, gaming areas, eXplorekid indoor playground and the popular Wild Wild Wet water park.

➕ e2 ✉ Pasir Ris Drive 3, next to Pasir Ris Park ☎ 6589 1688 🕐 Sun–Thu 10am–12.30am, Fri–Sat 10am–2.30am 🚇 Pasir Ris, then take shuttle bus

JOO CHIAT ROAD

The southerly section of this famous old strip is a fabulous place to sample the laid-back and casual side to Singapore nightlife, from cold beers on fold-away sidewalk tables to karaoke and girlie bars. It's sleazy in parts, but generally safe and a refreshing change from the downtown establishments. Head for the junction with East Coast Road.

➕ d3 ✉ Joo Chiat Road, junction with East Coast Road 🕐 Daily from dusk 🚇 Paya Lebar, then walk or take a taxi

MOOLOOLABAR

An unpretentious hangout with a relaxed Australian vibe and very friendly staff, Mooloolabar is a great place to relax at an outside table with a cool beer—they offer a great selection, including Stella Artois on draft. The food is classic pub type, such as burgers and pasta—try the spicy wings if you dare!

➕ M4 ✉ 20 East Coast Road ☎ 6440 0388 🕐 Daily 1pm–midnight 🚌 31, 76, 135, 196, 197

SINGAPORE INDOOR STADIUM

sportshub.com.sg

This stadium is home to many big sporting and live music events in Singapore. The ultramodern design includes a giant roof that resembles the Chinese character for the "lucky" number eight. Elton John, the Rolling Stones and the Harlem Globetrotters are among those who have played here.

➕ d3 ✉ Stadium Walk ☎ 6344 2660 🕐 Check events 🚌 11, 16, 608

DANCE CLUBS

As in most cities, Singapore dance clubs tend to suit particular groups of revelers. While the older expat crowds can be found at bars along Boat Quay, the younger set tend to hang around Club Street and Ann Siang Hill at bars like La Terraza Rooftop Bar. Nightclubs like the evergreen Zouk (▷ 51) attract both a local and international DJ-loving crowd.

EAST ISLAND ENTERTAINMENT AND NIGHTLIFE

Where to Eat

PRICES

Prices are approximate, based on a 3-course meal for one person.

$$$ over S$60
$$ S$30–S$60
$ under S$30

THE COASTAL SETTLEMENT ($)

thecoastalsettlement.com
This ultra-casual hideaway, surrounded by leafy tropical greenery, serves tasty takes on both Western and Asian dishes. Try the truffle mushroom linguine or beef rendang.

🔲 e2 ✉ Netheravon Road ☎ 6475 0200 🕐 Tue–Thu 10.30am–11pm, Fri 10.30am–midnight, Sat 8.30am–midnight, Sun 8.30am–11pm 🚌 29

EAST COAST LAGOON FOOD VILLAGE ($)

Great food and sea breezes make this popular. The satay is very good, as are the laksa and seafood dishes, including chili or black pepper crab.

🔲 d3 ✉ East Coast Parkway 🕐 Daily till late 🚇 Bugis, then bus 401 (Sat–Sun only)

FATCAT ICE CREAM BAR ($)

fatcat.sg
Dishes like charcoal waffles with egg yolk sauce and watermelon soju ice cream are just a few examples of the playful local twists FATCAT injects into sweet Western classics. The menu changes often.

🔲 d3 ✉ Blk 416 Bedok North Avenue 2, #01-25 ☎ 6241 0830 🕐 Mon, Wed–Thu 1–10, Fri 1–11, Sat 12–11, Sun 12–10 🚇 Bedok

JUMBO SEAFOOD ($$$)

jumboseafood.com.sg
You haven't eaten in Singapore until you've tried its famous chili crab and black pepper crab, and this open-air East Coast seafood shack is one of the best places to have them.

🔲 d3 ✉ 1208 East Coast Parkway ☎ 6442 3435 🕐 Daily 11.30–2, 6–11 🚇 Eunos, then bus 55 or 105 🚌 16, 55, 76, 135, 155

NO SIGNBOARD SEAFOOD ($$$)

nosignboardseafood.com
Originally a hawker stall with no sign-posting, the family-run brand has expanded to sit-down branches. The Geylang location is a great spot to enjoy chili crab and fresh fish from the tank.

🔲 K3 ✉ 414 Geylang Road ☎ 6842 3415 🕐 Daily noon–1am 🚇 Aljunied

RABBIT CARROT GUN ($)

rabbit-carrot-gun.com
Smashed avocado, red velvet pancakes and Scotch eggs are among the high-lights at this cozy British gastropub.

🔲 M5 ✉ 49 East Coast Road ☎ 6348 8568 🕐 Mon 11–10.30, Tue–Sun 8.30am–10.30pm 🚇 Dakota

SMOKEY'S BBQ

smokeysbbq.com.sg
From St. Louis-style pork ribs to pulled pork sliders and porterhouse steak, Smokey's whips up classic American barbecue favorites. Wash it down with a craft beer.

🔲 M3 ✉ 73 Joo Chiat Place ☎ 6345 6914 🕐 Mon–Fri 3–11, Sat 11am–midnight, Sun 11–11 🚇 Eunos 🚌 10, 12, 14, 16, 32, 40

STEAMBOAT

Not a form of transportation, rather a delicious method of tableside cooking where a selection of fish, meat and vegetables is placed in a container of boiling broth; you can cook it exactly to your liking then retrieve it with chopsticks.

Farther Afield

Singapore is so close to exciting Malaysian and Indonesian destinations that, if you have time, you should head to these neighboring cities, ports and islands to see how much difference a few miles can make.

MAL

Sembawan
Beach

Pulau
Seletar

Selat

Yishun
Park

Orchid
Country Club

Lower Seletar
Reservoir

Pulau
Punggol Barat

Johor

Pulau
Punggol Timor

Seletar
Airport

PUNGGOL

Pulau
Serangoon

Pulau Ubin

Mamam Beach

Chek Jawa
Wetlands

Desaru,
Rawa Island

TAMPINES   EXPRESSWAY

ANG
MO KIO

CENTRAL

SENGKANG

HOUGANG

HOUGANG ROAD

UPPER SERANGOON

PASIR
RIS

TAMPINES

Coney Island
Beach

Pulau
Ketam

Pulau Ubin
Park

Serangoon
Harbour

Pasir Ris
Beach

Pasir Ris
Park

Changi
Beach

CHANGI

EXPRESSWAY

TAMPINES AVENUE 10

LOYANG AVENUE

EXPRESSWAY

Changi
International
Airport

KALLANG-PAYA

LEBAR EXPRESSWAY

BISHAN

TAMPINES
RD

AVENUE

BARTLEY RD

Bedok
Reservoir

EXPRESSWAY

SIMEI

TOA
PAYOH

SERANGOON

EAST

PAN-ISLAND

NEW   UPPER   CHANGI   ROAD

CHANGI
EAST

BEDOK

ROAD

COAST

PARKWAY

SINGAPORE

EAST

EAST   COAST

East Coast Beach

Marine Cove

East Coast
Park

Pulau
Brani

MARINA COASTAL
EXPRESSWAY

entosa

ulau
ekukor

Pulau
Seringat

Pulau Tembakul (Kusu Island)

Pulau Lazarus (Sakijang Pelepah)

Pulau Sakijang Bendera
(St John's Island)

Farther Afield

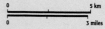

0   5 km

0   3 miles

Pulau Ubin

HIGHLIGHTS

● Groves of coconuts
● Old rubber plantation
● Mangrove swamps
● Hiking

TIP

● Be sure to take insect repellent and sunscreen, as well as a good hat.

This boomerang-shaped island, accessed via a short ride on a rickety bumboat from Changi Village, is filled with coconut groves, mangrove swamps and quiet temples waiting to be explored.

Wildlife and temples Pulau Ubin is a popular haunt for birdwatchers. Sightings of the red junglefowl, the wild ancestor of the domestic chicken, are fairly common, but if you're lucky you'll spot a rare hornbill. Wild boar and long-tailed macaque monkeys live here, too. Wildlife aside, there are some interesting Chinese temples here, including Wei Tuo Fa Gong (Lotus Temple) and Fo Shan Ting Da Bo Gong.

Chek Jawa This wetlands preserve is the most visited coastal area on the island. Here you can

Clockwise from far left: kampong houses on the beach; aerial view; rent a bicycle to explore the island; a local bungalow on the island

walk a 0.7-mile (1.1km) boardwalk that wraps around the verdant coast, and explore the rocky shoreline, mangroves and beaches—look for the sand bar where you'll find starfish, crabs and sand dollars at low tide. You can also climb up the 65ft-high (20m) observation tower for fine views toward Malaysia.

Eating and drinking Just off the jetty there is an endearingly scruffy little village with waterside restaurants where you refuel on Malay and Chinese foods, and refresh with a cold beer. This is also where you can rent a bicycle, which is the best way to explore the island. Elsewhere there are some drink stalls and vending machines scattered around the island, or do as most locals do and just pack a picnic lunch.

THE BASICS

nparks.gov.sg

➕ e2

🚇 Tampines, then bus 29 to Changi Village interchange. It's a 10-min bumboat ride from Changi Jetty (near the Changi Village Hawker Centre) to the jetty at Pulau Ubin. Bumboats operate from 6am to 11pm

✋ Bumboat ticket inexpensive

❓ Free guided walks organized by National Parks ☎ 6542 4108, 6545 4761

More to See

DESARU

On the eastern tip of the Malaysian peninsula, Desaru is a popular beach resort for Singaporeans, and a good introduction to Malaysian culture. Its clean, sandy white beaches are fringed by lush tropical forest. There are numerous resorts and hotels—activities include golfing, horse riding, tennis, canoeing, swimming, boating, fishing and snorkeling.

➕ See map ▷ 95 ✉ 78 miles (125km) northeast of Singapore. Accessible from Singapore by road via Kota Tinggi (2-hour drive), and by ferry from Changi Ferry Terminal. Daily sailings. Times vary; check easybook.com ☎ 6546 8518

RAWA ISLAND

rawaislandresort.com
alangsrawa.com

Within four hours of Singapore, this tropical private island off the east coast of Malaysia is popular for those looking for an escape from city life. Owned by sultan brothers who had different ideas on what to offer guests, the island is divided between Rawa Island Resort, a family-friendly place to stay with a dive center and waterslides, and laid-back Alang's Rawa, where guests will find bungalows on the beach with basic amenities and great home-cooked meals.

➕ See map ▷ 95 ✉ 120 miles (194km) northeast of Singapore. Hotels will arrange 30-min boat transfer from Mersing, Malaysia 🖐 Expensive

ST. JOHN'S ISLAND

Just 0.6 miles (1km) south of Sentosa, St. John's Island is a former penal settlement with idyllic, clean, sandy beaches, walking tracks and lagoons for swimming. The holiday bungalows, which can accommodate 10 people, have low rents and the picnic grounds are perfect for day-trippers.

➕ c4 ✉ 4 miles (6.5km) south of Singapore ☎ 6534 9339 🚢 45-min ferry ride from Marina South Pier. Departure times: Mon–Fri 10, Sat 9, 11, 1, 3, Sun 9, 11, 1, 3, 5 🖐 Expensive

St. John's Island

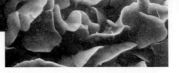

Diving Singapore's Islands

LEARN TO DIVE

Orpheus Dive Centre is a PADI 5-Star dive center offering scuba diving courses, ranging from beginner to professional levels. Weekly classes are held in Outram Secondary School's swimming pool, followed by ocean dives either around Singapore (where the visibility is not great) or on a two-day trip to Manado or Bali in Indonesia.
orpheusdive.com
☎ 6887 3631
✉ 16 Zion Road, Singapore

Some of Singapore's offshore islands are suitable for scuba diving, though guided tours are recommended due to the area's often strong currents. Local dive schools conduct NAUI or PADI courses with day and night diving options.

Kusu Island (Pulau Tembakul Kusu)

Kusu is one of the stops on the ferry loop from Marina South Pier. Its two swimming lagoons make it a popular destination for day-trippers. The warm fringing waters are ideal for swimming among hard and soft corals, pelagic fish, sea fans, sea snakes and turtles. Dolphins are sometimes seen as well.

As well as diving, you can visit the charming Da Ba Gong temple (Temple of the Merchant God), which attracts more than 100,000 devotees on the ninth month of the lunar calendar, and the Malay shrine Kramat Kusu. The short hike up to the hilltop is worth it for the stunning views of the mainland, too.

✚ Southeast of Sentosa
🚢 Ferry from Marina South Pier. Departure times: Mon–Fri 10, 2, Sat 9, 11, 1, 3, Sun 9, 11, 1, 3, 5
🎟 Return ticket S$18 adults, S$12 children 3 to 12 years
☎ 6534 9339
Average visibility: 3ft (1m). Maximum depth: 100ft (30m)

Six-banded angelfish (above) and a marine flatworm (above right)

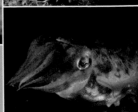

Squid

Lazarus Island and Sisters' Islands

These three tiny islands, just south of Singapore, have sandy beaches and are perfect for swimming, snorkeling and scuba diving. Since the currents are strong, divers should be experienced. On the southern tip of Lazarus Island there is a wreck at 60ft (18m). Sisters' Islands (Pulau Subar Laut and Pulau Subar Darat) are two little islands, which, legend has it, are two sisters who drowned while trying to escape from a pirate chief who wanted to marry one of them. Each island has shallow reefs and a bathing lagoon, but the current between the islands is swift and dangerous.

Lazarus Island

➕ Between St. John's Island and Kusu Island
✉ Causeway to St John's
💷 Return ticket S$9 adults, S$6 children 3 to 12 years
☎ 6534 9339
Average visibility: 3ft (1m)
Maximum depth: 60ft (18m)

Sisters' Islands

➕ South of Sentosa
🛳 Must charter ferry from Marina South Pier
☎ 6534 9339
Average visibility: 5ft (1.5m)
Maximum depth: 70ft (21m)

WATER

Traveling to the islands and getting around them is hot, thirsty work and you need to understand how to prevent dehydration and how to notice if you have it. On a hot day, it may take as little as 15 minutes to become dehydrated and the following are signs: dry lips and tongue, apathy and lack of energy, muscle cramping and bright-color or dark urine.

To prevent dehydration:
● Wear loose, light-color clothing
● Drink plenty of water
● Consume ample electrolytes (sodium and potassium dissolved in water)
● Cool off by pouring water over your head and neck

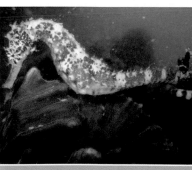

Tigertail seahorse

Icon seastar

Excursions

THE BASICS

brf.com.sg

🚢 Ferries leave Tanah Merah Ferry Terminal several times a day—the trip takes about 45 min

Bintan Resort Ferries

☎ 6542 4369

💰 Expensive

BINTAN

Bintan Island lies 28 miles (45km) southeast of Singapore, in the Riau Archipelago, the third-largest province of Indonesia. An excellent excursion from Singapore, the island provides an introduction to Indonesian culture; the friendly locals speak Bahasa Indonesia, but enjoy practicing their English.

North and south Numerous seaside resorts, hotels and chalets, catering to a wide range of budgets, cover the northern shores of the island and are separated from the rest of the island by checkpoints and security guards. The southern part of the island is more populated and industrial, with electronics factories, fishing villages and bustling towns with thousands of motorcycles.

Island life Tanjung Pinang is the largest town on the island. The old, central market area, built on stilts, is a fascinating place and small enough to walk around. Try the delicious local fruit and seafood, and browse the interesting shops and markets. Pulau Penyengat, a 10-minute bumboat ride from Tanjung Pinang pier, has a charming fishing village, the remains of an old palace, and a mosque dating from 1880.

Practicalities Local time is one hour behind Singapore time. Bring cash in rupiah for use in the shops and at street stalls; Singapore dollars and credit cards are sometimes accepted for accommodations and food. Make sure you have your passport and check to see if you need a visa for entry; most travelers can get a visa on arrival (US$15 up to seven days; $35 up to 30 days).

JOHOR BAHRU

Johor Bahru is at the southern tip of the Malay Peninsula, just a short ride across the causeway from Singapore. Also referred to as JB, the state capital of Johor is a thriving commercial and administrative center, with many shopping malls, hotels, restaurants and entertainment venues.

Choices Hotels in the city suit every taste and budget—there are resorts, international hotels and budget accommodations. Numerous nightclubs, karaoke bars and cinemas can be found in the heart of the city and, after sunset, a sumptuous array of food stalls appear along the streets. There are also plenty of hawker centers and restaurants offering traditional Malay, Indian and Chinese delicacies.

Shopping and sightseeing The favorable exchange rate and tempting bargains in the big shopping malls, handicraft centers, bazaars and markets make JB a popular shopping destination with Singaporeans and overseas tourists. The Royal Sultan Abu Bakar Museum (Grand Palace) and its immaculate gardens, the beautiful Sultan Abu Bakar Mosque and the Johor Art Gallery are some of JB's more famous historical and cultural attractions. The city is also a good point of departure for Malaysia's East Coast.

How to get there Take a Malaysian taxi from Rochor Road, where you can share a taxi, or book a specially licensed Singapore taxi. Buses run regularly from the Queen Street terminal near Bugis MRT stop. A ferry link also operates daily between Changi Point near the airport and Tanjung Belungkor in Johor. Most visitors will not need a visa but check beforehand.

FARTHER AFIELD EXCURSIONS

Pulau Ubin Sensory Trail

Pack sunblock and water, and head to the Sensory Trail, which displays Asian plants used for food, medicines and everyday items.

DISTANCE: 1 mile (1.5km) **ALLOW:** 60–90 min, best attempted early in the day

START

PULAU UBIN JETTY

e2 Tampines, then bus 29 to Changi Village. 10-min bumboat ride from Changi Jetty to the jetty at Pulau Ubin

❶ Walk through the little village that surrounds the jetty to the visitors' center, just a short distance from the jetty, on the right. Ask at the center for a map of the walk.

❷ The trail starts in the Spice and Herb Garden with a walk alongside a cool, shady banana grove. This useful plant is a good source of energy and vitamins and the leaves are used as food wrappers and disposable plates.

❸ The pathway continues past a huge field of fragrant pandan. The scented leaves are often used in Asian cooking for coloring and flavoring. Next are plantings of the grass citronella, long leafstalks of torch ginger, curry trees, climbing beans, passionfruit, guava, aloe vera, the elephant yam and finally a grove of sugarcane.

❹ The trail goes on to the second section of the walk, which takes you through coastal forest and mangrove habitat. Here you'll see spiky pandan (the leaves are used to make mats and baskets), mangrove trees, sea hibiscus (strings and cords are made from the bark), and betel nut palms (the nut is used in traditional Malay medicine).

❺ Next you'll visit the island's coconut plantations, where you can take a break and buy a cold drink or try some fresh coconut milk, straight from the coconut.

❻ Take the trail back to the center of the main village for a look around the shops, a fresh tropical fruit drink and a delicious seafood meal. Have a rest in the shade before you head back to the mainland.

END

PULAU UBIN JETTY

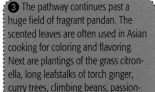

Shopping

TANJUNGPINANG CITY CENTER
Bintan's newest mall has a good variety of shopping, eating and entertainment options, including a hypermarket and Matahari department store.
➕ Off map ✉ Jalan Raya Dompak, Batu IX, Tanjung Pinang, Bintan ☎ 62 771 444 3522
🕐 Daily 9am–10pm

JOHOR BAHRU DUTY FREE COMPLEX (ZON)
zon.com.my
The largest duty-free complex in Malaysia offers electronics, clothing, alcohol and brand-name goods of all descriptions. Just 1.2 miles (2km) from the Singapore Causeway, ZON is easily accessible via daily ferry services from Tanah Merah Ferry Terminal.
➕ Off map ✉ 88 Jalan Ibrahim Sultan Stulang Laut, Johor Bahru ☎ 60 7227 4045
🕐 Daily 11–10 🚌 Regular buses from Customs area 6am–11pm

PLAZA PELANGI
A multitude of stores offer a wide array of quality merchandise, from handicraft items and souvenirs to fashion.
➕ Off map ✉ 2 Jalan Kuning, Taman Pelangi, Johor Bahru ☎ 60 7276 2216
🕐 Daily 10–10 🚌 Regular buses from Customs area 6am–11pm

Where to Eat

PRICES
Prices are approximate, based on a 3-course meal for one person.
$$$ over S$60
$$ S$30–S$60
$ under S$30

BANYAN TREE BINTAN ($$$)
banyantree.com
This luxury beach resort has three restaurants but the real attraction are the private candlelit meals for two by the South China Sea.
➕ Off map ✉ Bintan, Indonesia ☎ 62 770 693 100 🕐 Dinner daily from 6pm

NEW HONG KONG RESTAURANT ($)
nhkrestaurant.com
A popular Cantonese restaurant, housed in two shophouses with Oriental decor, specializes in dim sum and a variety of fish, poultry and vegetable dishes.
➕ b1 ✉ 69-A Jalan Ibrahim Sultan, Johor Bahru ☎ 60 7222 2608 🕐 Mon–Sat 11–3, 6–10

SEASON LIVE SEAFOOD ($$)
Sit at makeshift tables, sip fresh coconut juice and enjoy a seafood lunch of steamed king prawns, seafood soup and crabs fried with spicy black pepper.
➕ 2e ✉ 59E Pulau Ubin, Singapore ☎ 6542 7627 🕐 Daily 12–2, 5–10

TAMAN SRI TEBRAU HAWKER CENTRE ($)
Around 50 stalls sell JB's best Malaysian fare to be found under one roof. Try Penang-fried *kuay teow,* satay or Hokkien prawn *mee.*
➕ Off map ✉ Jalan Keris, Johor Bahru
🕐 Daily 10–10

Singapore has an abundance of hotels to suit every budget, from some of the region's finest five-star luxury properties to more affordable mid-range options.

Where to Stay

Introduction

It's no surprise that Singapore, which welcomes more than 12 million visitors a year (and counting), offers a full range of hotels for all budgets. The five-star luxury hotels are some of the best in Southeast Asia, and there are bargains to be had in the lower price tiers, as well. All are very well equipped and offer modern room facilities, while some of the more exclusive places have fitness centers, spas and excellent bars and restaurants.

Choice of areas

Singapore's mid-range hotels are scattered throughout the city center, and it is worth trying to find a hotel that suits your sightseeing tastes as much as your budget. Hotels located on or near Orchard Road provide easy access to retail and restaurants, while visitors with a keen interest in Singapore's vibrant local culture might look to Chinatown, Little India or Geylang. A number of luxury hotels surround glittering Marina Bay.

Reservations

Though Singapore is, of course, never fully booked, the best rates and rooms do fill up fast, so it's best to book online prior to your arrival; check Agoda.com for discounts. If you do arrive without prior reservations, the staff at SHA hotel reservation counters at the airport will help you find a place to stay. The STB's website (visitsingapore.com) also has a fantastic interactive booking service.

STAY AT THE AIRPORT

There are many reasons—delayed flight, lost booking, convenience—why you might like to stay at Singapore's international airport. Fortunately, three of the four terminals at Changi Airport have their own transit hotel, where for around S$80 per night you can rest in comfort, shower and change, swim in the pool, have a massage or use the business center, all without the hassle of immigration and customs clearance, and without worrying about getting to the airport to catch your next flight.

Singapore has a fantastic range accommodations for all budgets

Budget Hotels

PRICES

Expect to pay under S$100 per night for a budget hotel.

BROADWAY

broadway.bestsingaporehotels.net

The standards are high and the staff are friendly at this welcoming two-star hotel in the heart of vibrant Little India. Facilities are limited, but rooms come with complimentary tea/coffee supplies and satellite TV.

➕ F4 ✉ 195 Serangoon Road ☎ 6292 4661 🚇 Little India

CHAMPION HOTEL

championhotel.com.sg

Minimalist but stylish, this gem on pretty Joo Chiat Road offers rooms ranging from windowless singles to those with a tatami mat (and window). All accommodations include complimentary WiFi, toiletries and basic refreshments.

➕ M3 ✉ 60 Joo Chiat Road #01-06 ☎ 6342 0988 🚇 Eunos

HOTEL BENCOOLEN

hotelbencoolen.com

Conveniently located within walking distance of major sights and attractions like the National Gallery and Orchard Road, this boutique hotel offers comfortable, clean rooms, a small gym and daily breakfast.

➕ F5 ✉ 47 Bencoolen Street ☎ 6336 0822 🚇 Dhoby Ghaut, Bras Basah

KAM LENG HOTEL

kamleng.com

First opened in 1927, this smart hotel on lively Jalan Besar relaunched in 2012 with pastel-toned rooms. All rooms have a private bathroom, free WiFi and flat-screen TV.

➕ G3 ✉ 383 Jalan Besar Road ☎ 6239 9399 🚇 Lavender

RELC INTERNATIONAL HOTEL

relcih.com.sg

Just a 10-minute walk from the retail and dining pleasures of Orchard Road, this hotel offers a gym, laundry facilities and free WiFi. There's a room for all budgets and needs, too, from doubles to three-bedroom serviced apartments.

➕ C4 ✉ 30 Orange Grove Road ☎ 6885 7888 🚇 Orchard

STRAND

strandhotel.com.sg

Catering well to traveling couples and families alike, Strand is within walking distance of many of Singapore's top attractions and neighborhoods. WiFi is inclusive for all rooms, and there's a great café serving both local and Western dishes.

➕ F5 ✉ 25 Bencoolen Street ☎ 6338 1866 🚇 Dhoby Ghaut

TAI HOE HOTEL

taihoehotel.com

This no-frills hotel has a convenient location on Kitchener Road, offering easy access to the cultural districts of Little India, Jalan Besar and Bugis. The rooms are clean and comfortable.

➕ F3 ✉ 163 Kitchener Road ☎ 6293 9122 🚇 Farrer Park

YMCA INTERNATIONAL HOUSE

ymcaih.com.sg

This well-equipped YMCA, with a prime location near the start of Orchard Road, has a gym, swimming pool and dining options. Single, double and family rooms are available—book well ahead.

➕ E5 ✉ 1 Orchard Road ☎ 6336 6000 🚇 Dhoby Ghaut

Mid-Range Hotels

PRICES

Expect to pay between S$100 and S$400 per night for a mid-range hotel.

THE ELIZABETH SINGAPORE

theelizabeth.com

This well-located hotel has a small outdoor pool and fitness center, and there's something soothing about waking up to a breakfast served near the lobby's three-story-high series of waterfalls.

🔶 D4 ✉ 24 Mount Elizabeth ☎ 6738 1188 🚇 Orchard

FURAMA HOTEL SINGAPORE

furama.com/citycentre

There's a bright, modern look to this Chinatown hotel following renovations in 2017. Many rooms have fantastic views of the sparkling downtown core, and there's an outdoor pool, restaurants and fitness facilities.

🔶 E7 ✉ 60 Eu Tong Sen Street ☎ 6533 3888 🚇 Chinatown

HOTEL 1929

hotel1929.com

The 32-room boutique hotel was hotelier and restaurateur Loh Lik Peng's first contribution to the city. The rooms are small, but the artwork and prime Chinatown location make it a great pick.

🔶 E7 ✉ 50 Keong Saik Road ☎ 6347 1929 🚇 Chinatown

HOTEL CLOVER

hotelclover.com

Ranging from windowless singles to suites with outdoor whirlpools, all the rooms sport a modern, rustic design. It's in fashionable Kampong Glam, with its hookah lounges and Indian restaurants.

🔶 G4 ✉ 769 North Bridge Road ☎ 6340 1860 🚇 Bugis

HOTEL JEN TANGLIN SINGAPORE

hoteljen.com/tanglin

Make free international calls to 15 countries and get internet access on the complimentary smartphone all guests at Hotel Jen receive at check-in. Four bars and restaurants, a large outdoor swimming pool and great Orchard Road location are a few more reasons why this is a popular choice.

🔶 C4 ✉ 1A Cuscaden Road ☎ 6738 2222 🚇 Orchard

IBIS STYLES SINGAPORE ON MACPHERSON

ibis.com

The rooms are bright, airy and inclusive of a continental breakfast at this stylish hotel in Geylang, one of Singapore's best snacking neighborhoods. Free WiFi is available in the shared public areas.

🔶 K1 ✉ 401 Macpherson Road ☎ 6343 0088 🚇 Aljunied

NAUMI LIORA

naumiliora.com

To pay tribute to the heritage of these Perankan-styled townhouses, designers of this Chinatown hotel left details like the original timber flooring and French-styled windows intact. Coffee shops, bars and one of Singapore's hottest food scenes are at your doorstep.

🔶 E7 ✉ 55 Keong Saik Road ☎ 6922 9000 🚇 Chinatown

PARKROYAL ON PICKERING

singaporehotels.parkroyalhotels.com

A solar-powered sky garden, rain harvesting and LED bulbs are among the progressive eco-friendly initiatives undertaken at this striking Chinatown hotel. Spend an afternoon relaxing in the poolside cabanas or indulge in a treatment from the spa.

🏥 E7 ✉ 3 Upper Pickering Street ☎ 6809 8888 🚇 Chinatown

PENINSULA EXCELSIOR
ytthotels.com.sg
The facilities are a real draw here, particularly the two swimming pools, gym and sauna, as is its convenient location near expansive Fort Canning Park and nightlife hub Clarke Quay. The rooms are modern and spacious.
🏥 F6 ✉ 5 Coleman Street ☎ 6337 2200 🚇 City Hall

THE QUINCY
quincy.com.sg
Just off the Orchard Road, perks at this contemporary boutique hotel include inclusive in-room minibar, smartphone rental and airport lounge access. There's an outdoor infinity pool, too, and complimentary happy hour cocktails.
🏥 C4 ✉ 22 Mount Elizabeth ☎ 6738 5888 🚇 Orchard

SWISSÔTEL MERCHANT COURT, SINGAPORE
swissotel.com
This 476-room hotel, on the Singapore River between Clarke Quay and Chinatown, has extensive facilities that include a great pool, self-service laundry and a relaxing lobby bar.
🏥 E6 ✉ 20 Merchant Road ☎ 6337 2288 🚇 Clarke Quay

VILLAGE HOTEL ALBERT COURT
stayfareast.com
This handsome hotel features 210 rooms spread across eight floors of a beautifully renovated shophouse near Little India. All rooms have a walk-in rain shower and free WiFi.
🏥 F5 ✉ 180 Albert Street ☎ 6339 3939 🚇 Bugis

WANDERLUST
wanderlusthotel.com
Tucked away in a former schoolhouse in Little India, several local design agencies were given full creative freedom. The result is 29 unique rooms with such design themes as "space," "origami" and "typewriter."
🏥 E4 ✉ 2 Dickson Road ☎ 6396 3322 🚇 Little India

YORK HOTEL SINGAPORE
yorkhotel.com.sg
The York's spacious rooms are a little dated, but you can't beat the location just off Orchard Road. The 24-hour room service, babysitting service and lovely outdoor pool and sun deck with huge tropical palms are bonuses, too.
🏥 D4 ✉ 21 Mount Elizabeth ☎ 6737 0511 🚇 Orchard

YOTEL SINGAPORE
yotel.com
Geared towards millennials and business travelers, YOTEL offers smart features like self check-in and check-out, a 24-hour gym and, yes, even cheeky robot butlers. The rooms, here called "cabins," range from premium queen to VIP suite.
🏥 E8 ✉ 366 Orchard Road ☎ 6866 8000 🚇 Orchard

TRAVEL TO YOUR HOTEL

Besides Singapore's modern and efficient public transportation system, taxis are everywhere and very affordable. Another convenient way to travel to and from Singapore's Changi Airport is to take a six-seater MaxiCab shuttle service, which operates daily from 6am to midnight. The service has a flexible routing system between the airport and city hotels.

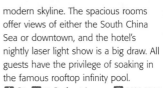

Luxury Hotels

PRICES
Expect to pay over S$400 per night for a luxury hotel.

FOUR SEASONS SINGAPORE

fourseasons.com/singapore

This five-star contemporary hotel is discreetly located just above Orchard Road. Facilities include a fully equipped spa, tennis courts and two outdoor pools, while the rooms feature Asian accents and furnishings.

⊞ C4 ✉ 190 Orchard Boulevard ☎ 6734 1110 ⊚ Orchard

THE FULLERTON HOTEL SINGAPORE

fullertonhotel.com

With its sweeping neoclassical architecture and imposing columns, you can't miss this historic hotel located in the heart of the Civic District. The 400-room luxury property occupies what used to be Singapore's General Post Office and is popular for its afternoon tea and swish cocktail club and rooftop bar.

⊞ F7 ✉ 1 Fullerton Square ☎ 6735 8388 ⊚ Raffles Place

MANDARIN ORIENTAL

mandarin-oriental.com/singapore

This five-star hotel has a classy, contemporary feel in both its serene public areas and its stylish rooms. The Marina Bay views can't be beaten, while nearby shopping centers include Suntec City and The Shoppes at Marina Bay Sands.

⊞ F6 ✉ 5 Raffles Avenue, Marina Square ☎ 6339 8811 ⊚ City Hall

MARINA BAY SANDS

The Marina Bay Sands and its unique curved three-tower structure has become an iconic landmark of the city's modern skyline. The spacious rooms offer views of either the South China Sea or downtown, and the hotel's nightly laser light show is a big draw. All guests have the privilege of soaking in the famous rooftop infinity pool.

⊞ G7 ✉ 10 Bayfront Avenue ☎ 6688 8868 ⊚ Bayfront

RAFFLES HOTEL

rafflessingapore.com

Relive the golden age of travel with a stay at Singapore's most famous (and gorgeous) heritage hotel, which first opened in 1887. Fully renovated in 2018, its old-world charm thankfully remains intact.

⊞ F5 ✉ 1 Beach Road ☎ 6337 1886 ⊚ City Hall

THE RITZ-CARLTON, MILLENIA SINGAPORE

ritzcarlton.com

Each of the rooms at this exceptional hotel come with dazzling Marina Bay views and large bathrooms with big octagonal windows. Equally impressive is the hotel's collection of 4,200 contemporary artworks—rent a self-guided audio tour—and its Michelin-starred Cantonese restaurant, Summer Pavilion.

⊞ F6 ✉ 7 Raffles Avenue ☎ 6337 8888 ⊚ City Hall

SHANGRI-LA

shangri-la.com

Now one of the world's top luxury brands, Shangri-La started with this flagship hotel in 1971. Enveloped in neatly manicured tropical greenery with a stunning outdoor pool, this refined hotel has fantastic restaurants, a world-class spa and luxurious rooms.

⊞ B3 ✉ 22 Orange Grove Road ☎ 6737 3644 ⊚ Orchard

Maximize your time in Singapore by planning ahead with a few essential tips on when to go, what to expect and more.

Need to Know

Planning Ahead

When to Go

The best time to visit Singapore is around Chinese New Year, although you will need to book a hotel well in advance. The annual Great Singapore Sale takes place from early June to early August. The city otherwise hums along year round, welcoming over 12 million visitors a year.

AVERAGE DAILY MAXIMUM TEMPERATURES

JAN	FEB	MAR	APR	MAY	JUN	JUL	AUG	SEP	OCT	NOV	DEC
86°F	88°F	88°F	89°F	90°F	90°F	87°F	88°F	88°F	88°F	88°F	86°F
30°C	31°C	31°C	32°C	32°C	32°C	31°C	31°C	31°C	31°C	31°C	30°C

Weather Singapore's climate is tropical, with very few seasonal variations. The temperature range is steady, from a nighttime low of 75°F (24°C) to a daily high of 88°F (31°C). December and January can be slightly cooler and April to June slightly hotter. Rainfall peaks between October and January, with the northeast monsoon. However, it rarely rains for long—usually an hour's torrential downpour at a time. During monsoon times, storms can be dramatic, with intense thunder and lightning. Most occur in the early morning and afternoon. Humidity can reach nearly 100 percent, and averages 84 percent.

WHAT'S ON

January *Art Stage Singapore*: Art from around the region is put in the global spotlight.
Thaipusam: This Hindu festival displays dramatic feats of mind over matter.
January/February *Chinese New Year:* A two-day public holiday, with fireworks, stalls and dragon dances.
February *Chingay Parade:* Street carnival based on a Chinese folk festival. Lion dancers, acrobats and floats.
March *Singapore Food Festival*
April *Singapore International Film Festival*

June *Dragon Boat Festival:* 20 teams enter this colorful longboat race.
Singapore Arts Festival: One of Asia's leading contemporary arts festivals.
July *Great Singapore Sale:* Singapore salutes all things retail every year from June to August with scores of markdowns and promotions.
August *National Day:* 9 August. This public holiday marks Singapore's independence from Malaysia.
August/September *Festival of the Hungry Ghosts:* Fun and feasting.

September *Mooncake Festival:* A colorful spectacle named after the delicious mooncakes on sale.
Singapore Grand Prix: Formula 1's only night race, held in Marina Bay.
October *Thimithi:* Firewalking ceremony.
October/November *Festival of the Nine Emperor Gods:* A week of processions and street opera.
November *Deepavali:* Lamps are lit to celebrate the triumph of good over evil.
December *Christmas:* Orchard Road lights up.

Singapore Online

Singapore is one of the most technologically advanced cities in Asia, and not surprisingly has a strong online presence.

visitsingapore.com

This dynamic site, written in more than 10 languages, is the official Singapore Tourism website and has up-to-date details of events, exhibitions, holiday ideas and shopping, dining and accommodations suggestions.

asiaone.com

This is the portal for Singapore's main media group. It includes links to all major national print media websites, plus international and regional news.

singapore.tourism-asia.net

There is plenty of up-to-date information on this site, with good sections on general travel, attractions, shopping and entertainment. The helpdesk section has useful practical information.

asiatravelmart.com

This is Asia's major online travel marketplace with various hotel and flight booking information, plus booking online.

nhb.gov.sg

Get comprehensive descriptions, photos and key information about historic sites, national monuments, museums and much more on the National Heritage Board's official website.

insing.com

Read restaurant reviews, catch up on local gossip, get shopping tips and find fun local events on this lifestyle site.

singaporeforkids.com

This website offers a light-hearted insight into unusual things to do both indoors and out, that will keep both kids and adults entertained.

TRAVEL SITES

fodors.com
A complete travel-planning site. You can research prices and weather; book air tickets, cars and rooms; ask questions (and get answers) from fellow travelers; and find links to other sites.

changiairport.com
Features arrival and departure details, airport facilities, and shopping and dining information in all terminals.

INTERNET ACCESS

All hotels offer internet access; some provide free WiFi.
Wireless@SG is a scheme that provides free wireless connection at selected hotspots. You will need a mobile device with WiFi facility, such as smartphone, laptop or tablet, and you have to register online with a service provider: iCELL (icellnetwork. com), M1 (m1net.com.sg) or SingTel (singtel.com). For the latest on Wireless@SG's coverage, see the IDA's website, ida.gov.sg.

Getting There

For airport inquiries
☎ 6595 6868;
changiairport.com.sg.

CAR RENTAL

● Car rental is expensive and public transportation is very good.

● An electronic road pricing system is installed in all cars, requiring rental drivers to pay Central Business District crossing line fees (during peak hours only).

● Display coupons in your windscreen in parking lots and designated parking places. Area day licenses and books of coupons can be purchased at newsagents, 7-Eleven and garages. Steep fines are incurred for failing to display licenses and coupons.

● Driving is on the left. A valid international or other recognized driver's license is required.

● Insurance is included in most rental fees.

AIRPORTS

Singapore's Changi Airport is 12 miles (20km) east of the city center. Flights take around 13 hours from Western Europe and around 20 hours from the US. The huge airport has four terminals, a movie theater, swimming pool and ample shops and dining options.

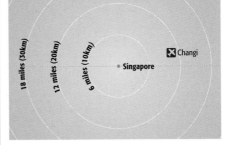

FROM CHANGI AIRPORT

Take the MRT train connection for easy access to all parts of the island. You can go to Tanah Merah station and switch to the westbound train service to be in the city in less than 30 minutes; the fare is less than S$2 (call 1800 336 8900 for inquiries).

Taxi ranks are well marked and lines move quickly. The fare into the city is around S$25.

The airport shuttle service (tel 6543 1985) stops at major hotels in the city (journey time 30 minutes; cost S$9). It runs 24 hours and can be picked up from just outside the terminal.

Public bus 36 travels to the city (6am to midnight; journey time 50 minutes; cost S$2). Pick it up below terminals 1, 2 and 3.

Car rental counters can be found in the Arrivals Hall of all three terminals and operate between 7am and 11pm.

ARRIVING BY BUS

Air-conditioned long-distance buses come direct from Bangkok, Penang and Kuala Lumpur, as well as from other main towns on the Malaysian Peninsula. To help make sense of the

many services operating routes between Malaysia and Singapore, visit Easybook (easybook.com), an online resource to compare fees and to locate the most convenient ticketing office and departure location. Buses between Singapore and Kuala Lumpur take around 6 hours, with prices starting at S$28. A bus ride to Bangkok takes around 28 hours, with fares starting at S$85.

Another website providing bus service information to and from Singapore is myexpressbus.com, covering companies that include Aeroline, Five Stars Travel, Grassland Express and Konsortium Express.

Odyssey (odysseynow.com.my) boasts leather recliners, wide leg room, a personal TV and meals for the journey from Singapore to Kuala Lumpur. Prices start at around S$40 each way.

Long-distance buses from Malaysia mostly arrive and depart from outside the Golden Mile Complex in Kampong Glam.

Bus 170 leaves the bus station at Johor Bahru (the Malaysian city visible across the causeway from Singapore) regularly for Queen Street bus station in Singapore (Singapore–Johor Bahru Express tel 6292 8149; journey time 1 hour; cost S$1.90). The Second Crossing, another causeway, links Tuas in Singapore's west with Malaysia's Johor state. All bus travelers break their journeys for immigration formalities.

ARRIVING BY SEA
Most cruise ships dock at the Marina Bay Cruise Centre. From there, taxis and buses go to central Singapore. Ferries travel regularly between Tanjong Belungkor (Johor) and Changi ferry terminal (Ferrylink, tel 6545 3600; journey time 45 minutes; cost S$25); to and from Tioman March to October (Auto Batam Ferries, tel 6271 4866; journey time 4 hours 30 minutes; cost S$120); and between HarbourFront and Bintan (Auto Batam Ferries, tel 6271 4866; journey time 1 hour 30 minutes; cost S$50).

VACCINATIONS
Vaccinations are not legally required unless you are coming from an area infected with yellow fever or cholera, but certain vaccinations may be advisable (for example hepatitis A and B) so check with your healthcare practitioner before traveling.

ENTRY REQUIREMENTS
Visas are not required by citizens of the EU, US or most Commonwealth countries (although Indian visitors staying more than 4 days require a visa). Passports must be valid for at least 6 months. On arrival, tourist visas are issued for 30 days. Extensions are available from the Immigration and Checkpoints Authority (app.ica.gov.sg ✉ 10 Kallang Road ☎ 6391 6100) or by making a trip outside Singapore. Passport and visa regulations can change at short notice, so always check before you travel.

AIRPORT HOTELS
Terminals 1, 2 and 3 have 73 transit hotel rooms each. Rentals are from S$77 per 6-hour block for single occupancy.

Getting Around

● Singapore Tourism produces lots of printed material about the island's attractions and tours and there are any number of brochures available from hotel reception desks. But the Touristline is handy for after-hours information and visitor centers are always worth a visit.

Touristline: ☎ 1800 736 2000 (toll-free in Singapore); +65 6736 2000 (overseas).
Chinatown: ✉ 2 Banda Street (behind Buddha Tooth Relic Temple) 🕔 Mon–Fri 9–9, Sat–Sun 9am–10pm 🚇 Chinatown

Orchard: ✉ Junction of Cairnhill Road and Orchard Road 🕔 Daily 9.30am–10.30pm 🚇 Somerset

● Overseas tourist offices: Australia Level 11, AWA Building, 47 York Street, Sydney, NSW 2000 ☎ 02 9290 2882/8
UK ✉ Grand Buildings, 1–3 Strand, London WC2N 5HR ☎ 020 7484 2710
US ✉ 1156 Avenue of the Americas, Suite 702, New York, NY 10036 ☎ 212/302 4861

BUSES

● Buses take exact change, though you can always give a dollar coin for a journey you know costs less.
● Buses are numerous and frequent. Buy individual tickets on the bus (exact change only), or use the ez-link card.
● Machines at the front of the bus take the card; press a button for the price of your particular journey. If you're not sure of the amount, ask the driver.
● A comprehensive bus and MRT timetable, called the Transitlink Guide, can be purchased at newsagents for S$1.50.
● Singapore Bus Service runs a hotline Mon–Fri 8–5.30, Sat 8–1. Tell them where you are and where you want to go. The telephone number is 1800 336 8900.
● SMRT Buses also operate a night service, called the NightRider, offering late or early morning travelers a safe and affordable means of travel. The fare for this service is S$3 per trip regardless of whether you are paying by cash or ez-link card. Concessionary travel is not available for this service.

MRT

● When Singapore's mass rapid transit (MRT) system is complete there will be six lines snaking across all corners of the island. Some lines and many stations are still under construction.
● Trains run between 5.30am and midnight.
● You can buy single tickets, but the one- to three-day unlimited Singapore Tourist Pass, starting at S$10 per day, is much better value. It can be used on buses as well as the MRT but not on premium services like the Sentosa Express or night buses.
● The ez-link card, also a stored-value card (minimum value S$10, plus a S$5 non-refundable card cost).
● Cards can be purchased from machines and from ticket offices. Tap them on machines at the barriers when entering and leaving stations.

● At the end of your stay refunds can be obtained on any amount outstanding on ez-link cards (but not the tourist pass).
● Useful numbers: MRT 1800 767 4333; MRT and bus integration 1800 336 8900.

TAXIS

● Taxis are easily found on Singapore's roads, though they can be more difficult to come by during rush hours (8am–9am and 5pm–7pm), just before midnight, and when it's raining.
● Shopping centers, hotels, sights and stations usually have taxi stands, and apart from these, taxis can also be hailed along the road. A taxi displaying a light at night is for hire.
● Taxis are air-conditioned and comfortable.
● Taxis charge a surcharge of S$3–S$5. There are surcharges for taxis hired from the airport, for fares between midnight and 6am, for bookings made in advance, for rush hours and for journeys via the business district or on roads where electronic road-pricing schemes are operating.
● Taxi drivers sometimes may not have sufficient change to accept large notes (S$50 or higher), so carry some low-value notes.
● Reserve in advance for important journeys, such as to the airport. Some taxi companies:
Comfort tel 6552 1111
Citycab tel 6555 1188
Comfort Premier Cabs tel 6552 2828
● Watch out for the Chrysler taxis, as the fare starts higher and also increases more rapidly.

TRISHAWS

● Singapore's trishaws are now confined to a few inner-city locations where they can be hired for a ride back in time. Tour operators will also organize group tours to the backstreets of Chinatown and Little India. Trishaw rides last an average of 30–45 minutes and cost from S$50 per person.
● Tour around Chinatown: Trishaw Uncle (trishawuncle.com.sg) offers tours around the city.

NEIGHBORHOODS

● Singapore's city neighborhoods—each one with a distinct character—are within easy reach by bus or MRT (Mass Rapid Transit). South of the river, Chinatown comes alive at festival time and just to the north is the CBD, with its tall office towers; across the river, the colonial district is set around the Padang, several museums and Raffles Hotel. Heading westward, busy Orchard Road is an international retail hub and along Serangoon Road, to the north, Indian culture thrives. Nearby Kampong Glam has long been at the heart of Malay culture. But try to discover some more out-of-the-way places, such as delightful Pulau Ubin, off the northeast of the island, or any one of the masses of public housing precincts where Singaporeans live.

VISITORS WITH DISABILITIES

Many hotels, shops and sights have facilities for people with disabilities, though getting around can sometimes be difficult because the MRT and buses are not wheelchair friendly. If you have a specific query, contact the National Council of Social Services ☎ 6336 1544.

Essential Facts

INSURANCE

Check your insurance policy and purchase supplementary coverage if necessary. Make sure you are covered for medical expenses.

MONEY

The unit of currency is the Singapore dollar. Brunei dollar notes have the same value as the Singapore dollar and are often accepted in Singapore. The Singapore dollar and other major currencies are easily changed to local currency in Malaysia and Indonesia. Traveler's checks are no longer widely accepted, so it's best to take a debit card.

EMERGENCY NUMBERS

● Ambulance and fire ☎ 995
● Police ☎ 999

MAGAZINES AND NEWSPAPERS

● The main English-language dailies are the *Straits Times*, the *Business Times*, *Today* and the *New Paper*. The latter is of a tabloid nature, seen as a fun alternative to others and as a result contains very little real news.
● The *International New York Times* is also available, as is a wide range of local and international magazines and publications.
● *Time Out Singapore*, *I-S* magazine and *Juice* are all good for listings.

MAIL

● Post office hours vary, but the post office at 1 Killiney Road is open Mon–Fri 9–5.30, Sat 9–1.30.
● Buy stamps in small shops and hotel lobbies, as well as at post offices.
● Postcards and airmail letters to all destinations cost 50 cents. The standard letter rate to Europe/US is S$1. Prepaid postcards and airmail letters are available.

MEDICAL TREATMENT

● Singapore's medical system is world-class. It offers a mixture of public and private treatment options. Make sure you have insurance cover.
● Many hotels offer guests a doctor-on-call service or can recommend a local doctor or clinic.
● If you require hospital treatment, you will need to provide proof that you can pay for it.
● The best centrally located hospitals are Mount Elizabeth (tel 6737 2666) and Gleneagles (tel 6473 7222). Both have emergency departments.
● Most medicines are available in Singapore.

MONEY MATTERS

● You can change money at the airport on arrival, or at hotels, banks and money-changers, who can be found all over town (and whose rate is slightly better than that given by banks and hotels). Most major banks have multiple branches across the Central Business District (CBD).

- ATMs are everywhere.
- Many shops, restaurants and hotels take credit cards.

OPENING HOURS

- Stores: hours vary widely but many are open 10–10. Most shops are open on Sunday.
- Banks: Hours again differ, but most banks are open Mon–Sat 9–3 and many branches are open on Sunday too.
- Offices: usually Mon–Fri 9–5; some open for half a day on Saturday and others open earlier and close later.
- Doctors' clinics: Mon–Fri 9–6, Sat 9–noon.

PUBLIC HOLIDAYS

- New Year's Day: 1 January
- Hari Raya Puasa: one day, January/February
- Chinese New Year: two days, January/February
- Good Friday: March/April
- Hari Raya Haji: one day, April
- Labour Day: 1 May
- Vesak Day: one day, May
- National Day: 9 August
- Deepavali: October/November
- Christmas Day: 25 December

TELEPHONES

- Phone calls within Singapore are very cheap—local calls cost as little as 10 cents for three-minute blocks.
- Phone cards for public phones (rare nowadays) can be purchased at stores and post offices.
- Calls from some hotels are subject to a 20 percent surcharge.
- International calls need to be prefixed by 001, followed by the country code. To call Singapore from outside, use country code 65.
- To reach the operator, call 100 for Singapore numbers and 104 for international numbers.
- If you don't have an international roaming plan for your phone, check whether your hotel offers smartphone rental.

EMBASSIES AND CONSULATES

- Australia ✉ 25 Napier Road ☎ 6836 4100 ◐ Mon–Fri 8.30–4
- Canada ✉ 1 George Street, #11-01 ☎ 6854 5900 ◐ Mon–Thu 8–4.30, Fri 8–1.30
- Ireland ✉ 541 Orchard Road, 08-00 Liat Towers ☎ 6238 7616 ◐ Mon–Fri 9.30–1, 1.30–4.30
- Malaysia ✉ 301 Jervois Road ☎ 6235 0111 ◐ Mon–Fri 8–5
- New Zealand ✉ 1 George Street, #21-04 ☎ 6235 9966 ◐ Mon–Fri 9–1
- Portugal ✉ 3 Killiney Road, #05-08, Winsland House 1 ☎ 6224 2256 ◐ Mon–Fri 9–1, 2–6
- Spain ✉ 7 Temesek Boulevard, #39-00, Suntec Tower One ☎ 6725 9220 ◐ Mon–Thu 9–1.30, Fri 9–1
- UK ✉ 100 Tanglin Road ☎ 6424 4200 ◐ Mon–Fri 8.30–5
- US ✉ 27 Napier Road ☎ 6476 9100 ◐ Mon–Fri 8.30–5.15

LOST PROPERTY

- Police ☎ 999
- For lost credit cards: American Express ☎ 1800 732 2566; MasterCard ☎ 1800 110 0113; VISA ☎ 1800 110 0344

Language

NEED TO KNOW LANGUAGE

Singapore has four official languages: English, Mandarin, Malay and Tamil, although a patois known as Singlish is often used (▷ 4). Nominally English, it uses words from other languages, primarily Malay and Hokkien Chinese. Its clipped phrases and stresses make interesting listening. Road signs, bus destinations and tickets all appear in English, and staff in stores, hotels and places of interest speak English. Here are some common Malay words and phrases.

USEFUL WORDS AND PHRASES	
selamat pagi	good morning
selamat petang	good afternoon
selamat malam	goodnight
selamat tinggal, selamat jalan	good-bye
api khabar?	how are you?
khabar baik	I'm fine
ya	yes
tidak	no
tidak apa	never mind
terimah kasih	thank you
sama sama	you're welcome
baiklah	OK
bila?	when?
esok	tomorrow
hari ini	today
semalam	yesterday
berapa har ganya?	how much?
mahal	expensive
murah	cheap
berapa jauh?	how far?
di mana?	where?
dibuka	open

NUMBERS	
satu	1
dua	2
tiga	3
empat	4
lima	5
sitta	6
tujuh	7
lapan	8
sembilan	9
sepuluh	10
sebelas	11
dua belas	12
tifa belas	13
dua puluh	20
tiga puluh	30
empat puluh	40
lima puluh	50
seratus	100
seribu	1,000

DAYS	
senin, isnin	Monday
selasa	Tuesday
rabu	Wednesday
khamis	Thursday
jumaat	Friday
sabtu	Saturday
ahad	Sunday

FOOD AND DRINK	
daging lembu	beef
ayam	chicken
ikan	fish
daging babi	pork
nasi	rice
nasi goreng	fried rice
mee goreng	fried noodles
sayur	vegetables
kopi	coffee
teh	tea

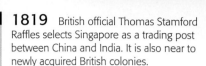

Timeline

EARLY DAYS

The first mention of Singapore comes in Chinese seafaring records of the 3rd century AD, where it is referred to as "Pu lou Chung" (island at the end of the peninsula). In the late 13th century Marco Polo noted a thriving city, possibly a satellite of the flourishing Sumatran Srivijayan empire. It could have been Singapore, then called Temasek. Sejarah Melayu (Malay annals of the 16th century) note a 13th-century Singapura (Lion City). In the late 14th century, the island's ruler, Parameswara, fled to Melaka. For 400 years Singapore was all but abandoned except for visiting pirates and fishermen.

Left to right: Sir Stamford Raffles, founder of Singapore; Raffles Hotel; plaque at the Former Ford Factory; Chinatown temple detail; an old newspaper at the Former Ford Factory; artwork at a Chinatown temple

1819   British official Thomas Stamford Raffles selects Singapore as a trading post between China and India. It is also near to newly acquired British colonies.

1826   With Penang and Melaka, Singapore becomes part of the British-run Straits Settlements.

1867   Singapore is designated a Crown Colony under British rule. It becomes a hub of international trade.

1870s Thousands of immigrants from south China begin arriving in Singapore. They work in shipyards and rubber plantations, and as small traders.

1887   Henry Ridley, director of the Botanic Gardens, propagates Asia's first rubber trees. Raffles Hotel opens.

1921   Japan's increasing military might causes the British to start building coastal defenses.

1942   Singapore falls to the Japanese.

1945   British Lord Louis Mountbatten accepts the Japanese surrender.

1954   Singapore's first elections: a legislative council is elected to advise the governor. Lee Kuan Yew helps found the People's Action Party (PAP).

1955 A Legislative Assembly is set up. David Marshall becomes Singapore's first chief minister.

1957 Malaya becomes independent. Singapore is a separate colony.

1959 PAP forms Singapore's first government, with Lee Kuan Yew as prime minister.

1963 Singapore forms the Federation of Malaysia together with Malaya, Sarawak and North Borneo.

1965 Singapore leaves the Federation to become an independent republic and joins the United Nations.

1966 The Singapore dollar becomes the official currency.

1968 The British announce military withdrawal. First parliamentary general election.

1990 Lee Kuan Yew steps aside, into the newly created post of senior minister.

2000 Singapore recovers from the Asian economic crisis.

2011 First presidential election, won by Tony Tan.

2017 Muslim Malay Halimah Yacob becomes Singapore's first female president.

JAPANESE OCCUPATION

In 1942 the Japanese launched their attack on Singapore. Despite being outnumbered three to one, they gained control of the colony in just a few days, during which time tens of thousands of British, Indian and Australian troops were killed or wounded. During the occupation up to 50,000 Chinese men were executed and the Allied troops were interned or dispatched to work on the infamous "Death" railway.

LEE KUAN YEW

Lee Kuan Yew is credited with transforming Singapore from a Third World trading port to a highly developed nation. Known for hard work and discipline, he encouraged developments in housing, education, infrastructure and manufacture, with amazing results.

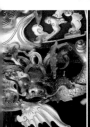

Index

127

Singapore 25 Best

WRITTEN BY Vivien Lytton
ADDITIONAL WRITING Rod Ritchie
UPDATED BY Brian Spencer
SERIES EDITOR Clare Ashton
COVER DESIGN Chie Ushio, Yuko Inagaki
DESIGN WORK Tom Whitlock and Liz Baldin
IMAGE RETOUCHING AND REPRO Ian Little

Published in the United Kingdom by AA Publishing

ISBN 978-1-64097-096-0

SIXTH EDITION

Color separation by AA Digital Department
Printed and bound by Leo Paper Products, China

10 9 8 7 6 5 4 3 2 1

A05593
Maps in this title produced from mapping © MAIRDUMONT / Falk Verlag 2013 and from data from openstreetmap.org © Open Street Map contributors
Transport map © Communicarta Ltd, UK

The AA would like to thank the following photographers, companies and picture libraries for their assistance in the preparation of this book:

All images courtesy of the Singapore Tourism Board except:

4tl AA/N Setchfield; 6cl AA/N Setchfield; 6c Buddha Tooth Relic Temple & Museum; 6bl AA/N Setchfield; 7cl Courtesy of Media Bank; 7c National Gallery of Singapore; 14tr Courtesy of Singapore Tourism Board (Danny Santos); 14tcr Courtesy of Singapore Tourism Board (Danny Santos); 17cl Courtesy of Singapore Tourism Board (Danny Santos); 18tr Courtesy of Singapore Tourism Board (1-Altitude); 18cr AA/N Setchfield; 19(i) AA/N Setchfield; 19(iii) AA/N Setchfield; 19(iv) Courtesy of The Hantu Blog; 20/21 Sebastian Duda/Alamy; 24tl AA/N Setchfield; 24/5t AA/N Setchfield; 24/5c AA/N Setchfield; 25r AA/N Setchfield; 26l Buddha Tooth Relic Temple & Museum; 26r Buddha Tooth Relic Temple & Museum; 27l AA/N Setchfield; 27c AA/N Setchfield; 27r AA/N Setchfield; 28l Paul Kingsley/Alamy; 28r Asia File/Alamy; 29r AA/N Setchfield; 30l Jeff Greenberg/Alamy Stock Photo; 30/1 Southeast Asia/Alamy Stock Photo; 32tl AA/N Setchfield; 35 Mikhail Pavlov/Alamy Stock Photo; 36l National Gallery of Singapore; 36r National Gallery of Singapore; 38/9 Horizon Images/Motion/Alamy; 39cr AA/N Setchfield; 40tl AA/N Setchfield; 40tr AA/N Setchfield; 42l Courtesy of Singapore Flyer Pte Ltd; 42r Courtesy of Singapore Flyer Pte Ltd; 43-46 AA/N Setchfield; 43bl AA/N Setchfield; 43br AA/N Setchfield; 44b AA/N Setchfield; 47 AA/N Setchfield; 48 AA/N Setchfield; 49 AA/N Setchfield; 50 AA/N Setchfield; 52-3 AA/N Setchfield; 54 AA/N Setchfield; 58/9 Courtesy of Singapore Tourism Board (Darren Soh); 60/1c AA/N Setchfield; 62 Courtesy of Singapore Zoo & Night Safari; 63t Courtesy of Singapore Zoo & Night Safari; 63cl Courtesy of Singapore Zoo & Night Safari; 63cr Courtesy of Singapore Zoo & Night Safari; 64 Courtesy of Singapore Tourism Board (Darren Soh); 66 AA/N Setchfield; 66/7t AA/N Setchfield; 66/7c AA/N Setchfield; 67tr Courtesy of Singapore Tourism Board (Maklin Ang); 67cr Courtesy of Singapore Tourism Board (Afur Wong); 69tr Courtesy of Singapore Tourism Board (Darren Soh); 70/1t Courtesy of Singapore Tourism Board (Marklin Ang);71r Courtesy of Singapore Tourism Board (Danny Santos); 72-76t AA/N Setchfield; 72bl AA/N Setchfield; 73b AA/N Setchfield; 74b Courtesy of Singapore Tourism Board (Afur Wong); 75bl Courtesy of Singapore Tourism Board (Afur Wong) 73br Courtesy of Singapore Tourism Board (Afur Wong); 76b Resorts World Sentosa; 78 AA/N Setchfield; 79 AA/N Setchfield; 81 AA/N Setchfield; 84tl Courtesy of Singapore Tourism Board (Danny Santos); 85tl AA/N Setchfield; 85tr AA/N Setchfield; 85c Courtesy of Singapore Tourism Board (Danny Santos); 86-87t AA/N Setchfield; 86bl AA/N Setchfield; 87b AA/N Setchfield; 88t AA/N Setchfield; 89 AA/N Setchfield; 90t AA/N Setchfield; 93 Courtesy of The Hantu Blog; 96l Courtesy of Singapore Tourism Board (Afur Wong); 96/97ct Courtesy of Singapore Tourism Board (Danny Santos); 96cb AA/N Setchfield; 97cr Courtesy of Singapore Tourism Board (Afur Wong); 98t AA/N Setchfield; 98b AA/N Setchfield; 99 AA/K Paterson; 100/101t Courtesy of The Hantu Blog; 100bl Courtesy of The Hantu Blog; 100cr Courtesy of The Hantu Blog; 100br Courtesy of The Hantu Blog; 101bl Courtesy of The Hantu Blog; 101br Courtesy of The Hantu Blog; 102t AA/R Strange; 102bl Leonid Serebrennikov/Alamy; 102br Leonid Serebrennikov/Alamy; 103t AA/N Setchfield; 103bl AA/N Hanna; 103bcl AA/N Setchfield; 103bc AA/N Hanna; 103bcr AA/N Setchfield; 103br AA/N Setchfield; 105 Courtesy of Singapore Tourism Board (Danny Santos); 106t AA/N Setchfield; 107 Courtesy of Singapore Tourism Board (Marklin Ang); 108-112t AA/C Sawyer; 108tr Courtesy of Singapore Tourism Board (Marklin Ang); 108tcr Courtesy of Singapore Tourism Board (Marklin Ang); 108cr AA/N Ray; 108br AA/N Setchfield; 123 AA/N Setchfield; 124bl AA/N Setchfield; 124bc AA/N Setchfield; 124br AA/N Setchfield; 125bl AA/N Setchfield; 125bc AA/N Setchfield; 125br AA/N Setchfield

Every effort has been made to trace the copyright holders, and we apologise in advance for any accidental errors. We would be happy to apply the corrections in the following edition of this publication

Titles in the Series